HISTORY OF SALVATION

HISTORY OF SALVATION

Introducing the Old Testament

JOHN POWER, S.M.A.

alba house DIVISION OF THE SOCIETY OF ST. PAUL
STATEN ISLAND, N.Y. 10314

© John Power, S.M.A., 1967

Cum permissu superiorum: John Creaven, S.M.A.

Nihil obstat: Michael Grace, S.M.A.

Imprimatur: ✠ Eugenius
Epus. Dromoren.,
Die 8 Novembris, anno 1966.

Alba House is staffed by the Pauline Fathers and Brothers
of the Society of St. Paul, Staten Island, New York, as a
part of their publishing apostolate. The Society was founded
to spread the teachings of Christ by means of the press,
radio, motion pictures and television.

Printed and Bound in the Republic of Ireland by Hely Thom Limited

Contents

Author's Foreword

THIS book began as a course of lectures on the Old Testament given to the Catholic teachers of the diocese of Dromore during the academic year 1964–5. The lectures were due to the insistence and encouragement of Fr Peter McConville, Dromore, to whom I owe much gratitude for his patient and practical "stage-managing" of the course. The book is largely the result of the teachers' repeated requests for a permanent copy of the lectures. Only slight alterations have been made in the text, and two chapters have been added.

The author and publishers are grateful to the Editor of *The Furrow* for permission to reprint " The Paschal Lamb " which was first published in that journal in slightly different form.

Introduction

THE aim of this book is to present, as briefly as possible, the background information necessary for a fruitful reading of the Old Testament. It is the minimum information. This is strictly a book for beginners. Fortunately, we have finally come to realize that, as far as the Old Testament is concerned, so many of us are beginners. And with this realization has come a great hunger for more knowledge about it—its contents, its message, its meaning, its relevance. This desire to know, understand and use the Old Testament is one of the most consoling aspects of the biblical revival of the present decade. That a book as elementary as this seems necessary is an indication of the sparseness of our knowledge; that people may be willing to read it is a tribute to their serious desire to know the word of God.

What is the minimum information that must be provided in order to make the reading of the Old Testament intelligible and interesting? This is not an easy question to answer. Our main object has been to present an outline of the story—the sequence of events. It is easy to show that these events were not haphazard or accidental, but that the Old Testament moves forward towards a climax, the incarnation. No man is born into a vacuum, and Christ was not born into a vacuum. The Son of God entered the stream of human history at a definite point in time. The function of the Old Testament is to demonstrate how time, persons and events prepared for and pointed to the incarnation.

There has been, frankly, no attempt at completeness. The intention has been to lead people to read the Old Testament itself, and to enjoy reading it. A mass of information can sometimes prove a road-block rather than a signpost to the biblical text. There is, for example, no treatment of the messianic theme, so rich and so constant in the Old Testament. But we understand and appreciate the messianism of the Old Testament only in the light of its fulfilment in the New, and it can be dealt with in a more satisfactory manner in the context of the New Testament. Perhaps there is a little over-simplification at times; the guiding principle has been that it is better to arouse interest by giving some information rather than bewilder by giving too much.

The Old Testament is not as difficult as it is sometimes made to seem. The Bible is not an impossible book, and the fruitful reading of it does not necessarily involve specialized training or an expensive library. An understanding of the Bible does not consist in prolonged and painful explanations of tiny passages, but in having a general picture of the biblical story that is perfectly clear. The Bible is the word of God, and God's word was not intended to be the monopoly of scholars. The plain fact is that the Bible is a book for everybody, not merely for highbrows, crackpots or mystics. Just as redemption is for all men without exception, so revelation and inspiration are for the benefit of all humanity. The Bible is a gift of God to men, distributed with divine largesse, unsparingly and to all. We need to remove from the Bible the aura of false mystery that has surrounded it for too long; we need to convince ourselves that the Bible is a book written for, and with a message for, every Christian.

What is this message? Surely it is the stunning story of how much God loves men, and how he has continued to love them in spite of their frailty. This is not the story of a hidden and aloof deity, but of a God who speaks to men in their own way and their own words, who is loving enough and patient enough to accommodate himself always to the weakness and shortsightedness of men.

Just as God is not a hidden God, so his love is not an intangible abstraction. It shows itself in action in the lives of men and nations. God not alone loves, but proves his love by giving. We can see his love as a pattern in history, a divine plan to bring God and men close together. The unity of the Bible, Old Testament and New, is based on the fact that all of it, from the creation in

Genesis 1 to the final consummation in Apocalypse 22, is the story, in successive stages, of this divine plan by which the love of God has been poured out on men. The slow working-out of that plan is what we call Salvation History.

While all other history deals with the relations between man and man, salvation history has the sole aim of describing relations between God and man. By its very nature, it is a theology of history. It is history meditated on, prayed about and prayed for; it is history viewed in the light of faith. This, of course, doesn't make it any less historical, but it does make it different from secular history.

Salvation history, however, is real history, that is, it is a real-life drama of events and people. It is not a theory, an opinion, a formula, a belief, a set of morals or dogmas. It has the very stuff of human life in it; it teems with people just like us; there are no lifeless abstractions in the pages of the Bible. This is a flesh-and-blood story, but a flesh-and-blood story in which God has mixed and mingled. And that is why salvation history is completely relevant to our day and to every man. Because we are men, we are part of history, and because Christ died for us, we are part of salvation history. The Bible is not the story of the salvation of others; it is the story of *our* salvation.

Our first concern, then, in reading the Bible shall be to form in our minds a clear outline of the historical sequence, a total vision of the salvation story. And it is well to begin by trying to see it all, New Testament as well as Old, so that we can then proceed to put the Old Testament in its proper Christian perspective.

As the Bible presents it, the story of salvation takes the form of a continuous divine activity in three well-defined stages.

STAGE 1 : God at work in the world—in the life of Israel; this is the story of the *Old Testament*.

STAGE 2 : God at work in the world—in the life of Christ; this is the story of the *Four Gospels*.

STAGE 3 : God at work in the world—in the life of Christians; this is the story of the *Acts of Apostles* and the *New Testament Epistles*.

STAGE 1: God at work in the world of men in and through Israel—this is the only idea that will bring unity and order to the books of the Old Testament, so diverse in style, content and purpose. The divine plan of redemption really takes definite shape and direction with the call of Abraham. This call is described in Genesis 12. All that the Bible says before that is merely an introduction—a prologue to the salvation story. Genesis 12 presents us with God's loving call and Abraham's generous response. An introduction is necessary to put this incident in its proper perspective. This introduction will have to explain: who and what this God is; who and what man is; what relationship there is between God and man; man's miserable condition and God's obvious affection for him. This is what the first eleven chapters of Genesis do; they tell of the creation of the world and of man by God, the frailty and fall of man, the repeated punishments and pardons that came to men from God. They give us the prologue to the story of salvation.

With the call of Abraham God's slow courtship of fallen man really begins. Following this divine call, a single family left Mesopotamia in the nineteenth century B.C. Some 600 years later, it had grown into a large and grumbling group of slaves suffering under a tyrannical Pharaoh in Egypt. At this point salvation history takes a great leap forward, because God, acting through Moses, achieves one of his dramatic saving interventions in history—the exodus. Joined to the exodus incident is the covenant of Sinai, in which the Israelites are welded together into a single people by their common allegiance to one God. But a people, in order to survive, to continue, must have a territory to call their own, and so the next step in the narrative is the entry into Palestine, the land God has promised them. This is achieved under the leadership of Joshua. However, a people in a land need a principle of unity, need one man as leader and co-ordinator, and thus the people and their land become a kingdom. And the name to be forever associated with the kingdom is that of David. Many of David's successors were unfaithful and unworthy kings, and a divided kingdom stumbled on its way to ultimate dissolution. The Babylonian captivity in the sixth century was their providential chastisement, and from the exile a little group returned to Jerusalem to rebuild the shattered heritage of their faith. Under the leadership of Ezra they formed themselves into a little community of believers clustered around the rebuilt Temple. No longer a kingdom, they are now a community of worshippers of God, what we could call a church.

This, in sketchy outline, is how God worked through his people in the Old Testament. He watched over Israel as it grew from a single Patriarch into a race. As we read the Old Testament, we shall see Israel pass through the successive stages of being a family (under Abraham), a people (under Moses), a land (under Joshua), a kingdom (under David), and a church (under Ezra). But all the time, and through all these stages, they looked forward to a golden age in the future, to a dim vision of a messianic era and a messianic kingdom. In this way, the Old Testament ends without being completed; it points to something beyond itself; it is clearly "to be continued".

STAGE 2: God at work in the world through his Son. The incarnation was the final coming of the long-promised and long-awaited One. Christ himself took pains to show, by word and act, that he is the crown and completion of the Old Testament story. We shall see how, in the Sermon on the Mount, he fulfilled the law. Taking the ancient Sinai decalogue, he explained its full meaning. "You have heard that it was said to the men of old . . . But I say to you . . ." This is what he meant when he assured his audience:

Think not that I have come to abolish the law and the prophets; I have come not to abolish them but to fulfil them (*Matt.* 5:17).

In his teaching he fulfilled the law, that is, he revealed its true meaning and extent, and in every aspect of his life and death he fulfilled the prophets. They had foretold him as suffering and yet triumphant, and in his death and resurrection the paradox of Isaiah became clear—the Suffering Servant is also a gloriously reigning king.

Now, if we look a little closer, we shall notice that the evan-

gelists, in writing down the story of Christ, describe his career
in a manner that is a perfect parallel with the Old Testament
narrative. They tell us of Christ's birth, his hidden years, his
public witness, his suffering, and finally his resurrection. This is
exactly how the Old Testament story had been constructed. It
tells us of the birth of the people of God at Sinai, and then of the
hidden years of the young nation as it struggled to gain a toe-hold
in the Promised Land under Joshua and the Judges. Next comes
the foundation of the kingdom, and Israel is established among
the nations of the orient as a public witness to her God. After
that, Israel's passion—her chastisement and purification through
exile, opposition and obscurity. And finally, the resurrection—
into the new Israel of God, the Church of the New Testament.
Thus the two Testaments dovetail to form an unbroken continuity
in the salvation story.

However, the coming of Christ was much more a beginning
than an end. Besides being the end of humanity's long vigil for a
redeemer, it was a new beginning, the beginning of the Messianic
era that will continue until Christ's second coming in clouds of
glory. Thus the Gospels, like the Old Testament, are incomplete;
they too are "to be continued".

STAGE 3: God at work in the world in the life of Christians
and the Church. Christ had pronounced himself the Way, the
Truth and the Life, and this statement lost none of its force by
his ascension. The Acts of the Apostles and the Epistles point out
in detail how Christ continued to be Way, Truth and Life for the
infant Church. He continued to be the Way to God by the norms
of Christian charity and Christian living he had laid down—love
of all men, patience under persecution and scorn. He continued
to be Truth, through the teaching of a Church guided and
guarded by his Spirit. He continued to be Life, through the
sacraments, which fed, sustained and strengthened his followers.
It is so clear from the Acts, which is really the first thirty years
of Church history, that the infant Church is simply Christ living
on in the world, doing now through his mystical body what he
had done in Galilee and Jerusalem through his physical body.

And it is easy to see that the second part of the New Testament —Acts, Epistles and Apocalypse—reveals the same general design that we have seen in the Old Testament and the Gospels. Because these books describe the birth, hidden life, public witness, suffering and resurrection of the Church and its members. The birth of the Church at Pentecost is presided over by the same Spirit who had inaugurated the people of God at Sinai, and had overshadowed Mary in the conception of Christ. This is followed by the hidden life of the Jerusalem Church, described in the first chapters of Acts. Next, there is the public witness, opening up dramatically in Acts 9 and 10 with the conversion of Paul and the reception of Cornelius. The Church now begins its task of going out to profess Christ and him crucified before the huge pagan empire. The suffering comes quickly and surely, and Acts 12 records Herod's persecution and Peter's imprisonment—the first of many. But the New Testament ends on the note of resurrection —the final glorious one described in the Apocalypse, the faithful around the throne of the Lamb.

Thus, the three stages of the salvation story follow the same pattern—from frail beginning to ultimate glory, from human weakness to the kinship of God. This is the unity of the Bible, the harmony between the two testaments. It really is the story, on a universal scale, of every human life—from birth to the beatific vision. This, then, is salvation history, and this is what the Bible sets out to give us.

Now we can turn to the Old Testament, knowing that, as we read it, we are tracing the hand of God through human history. To read the Old Testament, and to think over it, is to be stunned by God's tremendous love for men. It is the story, not merely of a God who revealed himself to men, but of a God who gave himself to men. But to see and savour this fully, we must *read the Old Testament*. We must read the biblical text, rather than read about it. It is never enough to read a synopsis of it, or an explanation of it. Obviously, the words of men can never be an adequate substitute for the word of God. This little book is simply an attempt to make the reading of the Old Testament text an easier, more interesting and more enriching experience.

The scriptural quotations throughout are from the Revised
Standard Version. This is one of the best English translations of
the Old Testament that we possess. Those accustomed to the
Douay Version will, however, notice that the use of the Revised
Standard Version results in some unfamiliar elements. The most
obvious of these are:

(1) The spelling of personal names, e.g.

RSV	DOUAY
Elijah	Elias
Isaiah	Isaias
Micah	Micheas

The Revised Standard Version spelling is closer to the original
Hebrew words, because the Douay reproduces the Greek spelling
of the Septuagint.

(2) The numbering of the Psalms. The Douay Version and the
Roman Catholic liturgy follow the numeration found in the
Septuagint, but the Revised Standard Version uses that of the
Hebrew text. This means that, from Psalm 9 to Psalm 147, the
numbering of the Revised Standard Version will be normally one
above that of the Douay, e.g. Psalm 29 (RSV) is Psalm 28 (Douay).
Perhaps the easiest way to explain this is to give the comparative
numbering of the two translations.

	RSV	DOUAY
Pss.	1–8	1–8
	9–10	9
	11–113	10–112
	114–115	113
	116	114–115
	117–146	116–145
	147	146–147
	148–150	148–150

(3) Some of the Old Testament books receive titles different
from those used in the Douay, viz.

RSV	DOUAY
1 Samuel	1 Kings
2 Samuel	2 Kings
1 Kings	3 Kings
2 Kings	4 Kings
1 Chronicles	1 Paralipomenon
2 Chronicles	2 Paralipomenon
Ezra	1 Esdras
Nehemiah	2 Esdras
Song of Solomon	Canticle of Canticles

CHAPTER 1

An Inspired Book

As we go along, we shall see that the formation of the Old Testament was a long process, and a human process. We shall be fully convinced that the Bible did not tumble readymade down from heaven, announcing mysterious words in archaic and sonorous English. But this human element in its origin does not explain why this ancient book is still, after more than 2,000 years, the world's best-seller. We begin, then, by turning our attention to that aspect of the Bible which makes it entirely unique among all documents ever written—its divine inspiration.

"Inspiration" is a word that we use rather loosely in contemporary English. We speak of poetic inspiration, artistic inspiration, even of the inspired words of a politician who guesses the future more shrewdly than his fellows. But here we are speaking of inspiration in a strictly limited sense, that is, biblical inspiration. Now, biblical inspiration means a special divine assistance given to a man by which he is enabled to transmit a message from God in written human words. Inspiration, then, involves three elements: God, a man, and a book, and to understand it we shall take account of each of these three in turn. But first let us look at the fact of inspiration and see how our conviction of it arose.

The Church has always accepted and taught the inspiration of the books contained in our Bible. The Church, as far as inspiration is concerned, makes no distinction between the Old Testament and the New, or between one book and another. It regards all the books of both testaments as equally inspired, as written by men under God's special guidance.

As we read the Old Testament we shall become aware of two facts:

Firstly, the Israelites knew that God had chosen them, and that the salvation story was being worked out through them. They saw history as *a series of interventions by God*. They tended to ignore secondary causes and to attribute all the incidents of their career directly to God. He brought them out of Egypt, he spoke to them at Sinai, he guided them through the desert, he led them across the Jordan, he laid low the walls of Jericho. They saw his hand at work on every side; they knew that they were being guided and guarded by his will and his words. And in all this they were correct.

Secondly, we become aware that *God's will and God's words came to them through men*. At every stage in their history God raised up leaders in Israel who spoke in his name and announced his wishes. He spoke first through the Patriarchs, then through Moses and Joshua, later through the Judges and the Kings, and most dramatically of all through the Prophets. Israel understood that the life and words of these men had brought her the words and the will of God. As God said to Jeremiah:

"Behold, I have put *my* words in *your* mouth" (*Jer.* 1:9).

Therefore, through the history of their nation and the preaching of their prophets they heard the voice of God. And since it was the voice of God, it deserved to live, to continue, to sound in the ears of generation after generation of the children of Israel. This could be done effectively only by putting it finally into a fixed, written form. And they continued to regard these written words with the same reverence, because these words were still the voice of God. Thus, the prophets who preached and the scribes who wrote down their preaching, the kings who ruled and the chroniclers who wrote of the kings, all spoke for God, and all had some share in God's guidance of his people. Israel thus became conscious that the activity of writing these books was another aspect of God's intervention in history; this literary activity was part of the guiding providence of God that had led them from the tents of the Patriarchs to the Temple of Jerusalem. And so

was born the idea of divine inspiration. That is why we find the
New Testament referring to the whole Old Testament simply as
"the word of God".

Christ, in speaking to his fellow-Jews, ratified their reverence
for the Old Testament. He asked them: ". . . have you not read
what was said to you by God . . ." and went on to quote Exodus 3.
To read the Old Testament was to read "what was said to you by
God". The Apostles, in their initial preaching of the Gospel,
followed their Master's example; in the first chapter of Acts,
St Peter says that "the holy Spirit spoke beforehand by the mouth
of David", and proceeds to quote from several Psalms.

As was his custom, St Paul brought more clarity and precision
to the idea. He wrote to young Timothy, his favourite convert:
". . . from childhood you have been acquainted with the sacred
writings which are able to instruct you for salvation through faith
in Christ Jesus. All scripture is inspired by God and profitable
for teaching, for reproof, for correction, and for training in
righteousness, that the man of God may be complete, equipped
for every good work" (2 *Tim.* 3:15-17).

"All scripture" here means all the Old Testament—the New
Testament had not yet been written when Timothy was a boy.
But a letter written ten years later puts the Epistles of St Paul on a
par with the Old Testament. St Peter, in his second Epistle, tells
his new Christians: ". . . our beloved brother Paul wrote to you
according to the wisdom given him, speaking of this as he does
in all his letters. There are some things in them hard to understand,
which the ignorant and unstable twist to their own destruction,
as they do *the other scriptures*" (2 *Pet.* 3:15-16).

From such little phrases we can conclude that a body of early
Church writing was being assembled, and that it enjoyed, in the
minds of the Apostles, the same honour and the same position as
the Old Testament. And St Paul has given a name to that position
—these writings are "inspired by God". That means that they
have been breathed into by God, in-spirited by God, are the
product of the breath or spirit of God. To say the same thing in
our more theological language—these books, whether history,
law, prophecy, psalm, wisdom or pastoral letter, have been

written with special help from the holy Spirit, God's beam of light on human minds. From Paul's time onward this unique relationship of God, man and book is known as inspiration.

Canon of Scripture

The infant Church of the apostolic age had, then, the duty of gathering together the inspired books of both Testaments and handing them on as the word of God. This, like the composition of these books, was not an instantaneous and semi-miraculous process; it was a slow patient work. It involved sifting the wheat from the chaff, accepting some books as inspired, and rejecting many others then in circulation. The list of the books accepted is called the Canon of Scripture, and it forms the index to our Bibles. The rejected ones are the books we now call Apocryphal, books with such titles as: Gospel of Thomas, Assumption of Mary, Preaching of Peter, Letters of Paul and Seneca, Apocalypse of Stephen.

How did it come about that the Church took upon itself this task of assembling and identifying the inspired books? Perhaps we can put it like this. Christ's decision to found an enduring Church included all the means necessary to enable this Church to endure and to fulfil its divine function in the world. One of these means was a body of writing by which the Church could be recognized and understood, and by which it could transmit God's words and intentions to mankind, at all stages of the human race and to all national groups. Christ's guidance of the early Church manifested itself in the Church's ability to recognize and accept the books inspired by the same divine guidance.

This helps us to see the true relationship between the Bible and the Church. The books of the Bible did not become inspired because the Church included them in its canon; rather they are included in the canon because they are inspired. Only God can inspire an author, but he left to his Church the more pedestrian task of identifying which books he had inspired. And it is also possible to see, from this vantage-point, how all these activities that surrounded the growth and formation of our Bible are really different manifestations of God's presence to his chosen ones—in the old Israel and in the new. It is the guiding Spirit of God who inspired the writers of the Old and New Testaments; it is the same guiding Spirit of God who enlightened the Church in the assembling of the inspired books. The drawing-up of the Canon of Scripture was an enterprise mantled by Christ's promise: "I am with you always, to the close of the age."

Now we turn to the process of writing an inspired book. We have said that three elements must be taken account of: God, man, book—God as the source of inspiration, a man as the subject of inspiration, and a book as its terminus.

God

The activity of God in inspiration is best described in the words of Pope Leo XIII in his encyclical *Providentissimus Deus*, the text of which is found at the beginning of many Douay Bibles. He expresses it like this: "By supernatural power, he (God) so moved and impelled them to write—he was so present to them—that the things which he ordered, and those only, they, first, rightly understood, then willed faithfully to write down, and finally expressed in apt words and with infallible truth." The first constituent of inspiration, then, is that God impels a man to write a book. But there are many ways in which God can do this. It need not involve a miraculous and sensational command—a voice from on high thundering in the night. God can impel a man to write by providing him with a natural motive for writing, by using circumstances and other men to prompt or oblige a man to write. Thus, it is possible for a man to write under inspiration without being aware of his inspiration. For example, we have no indication from St Paul's Epistles that he knew he was writing inspired documents. Paul wrote his first Epistle to Timothy probably in A.D. 65. We are justified in saying that, as he wrote it, he never for a moment suspected that this letter would be read in A.D. 1965 by people living in a barbaric island Paul had never heard of, because Hibernia lay beyond the western frontier of his Roman Empire.

In attempting to explain the activity of God in inspiration, theologians have always applied to it the theory of instrumentality, the theory that God uses the human author as an instrument with which to write a book. When we go to the blackboard we use chalk as an instrument with which to write a word. Now, has that word been written by the teacher or by the chalk? The answer is by both, each contributing something distinctive. Without the chalk, the teacher could not have written; without the teacher, the chalk could not have written. But the teacher and the chalk are not equals; the teacher used the chalk as a subordinate instrument; the chalk did not use the teacher. To borrow the philosophers' language, the teacher is the *principal cause* of the writing, the chalk is an *instrumental cause*. Something similar happens in inspiration. God takes a human being, and uses him as an instrument with which to write a particular book. But God and the man are not equals; God is the principal author of the inspired book, man an instrumental or secondary author. But they both share authorship of the completed book, and of every part of it, even the apparently insignificant passages. To return to the word on the blackboard—it is not true to say that the teacher alone wrote part of it and the chalk alone wrote another part of it. Similarly with the Bible. God is the author of all of it, the simple and the sublime; and man is the secondary author of all of it, the great flashes of wisdom and the tiny historical details.

Man

What happens to a man when this divine aid known as inspiration moves him to write? Here again we take up the image of the instrument, the chalk in the teacher's hand. The chalk enables the teacher to write a word, but the chalk also limits the kind of word the teacher can write. If the chalk is white, the writing will be white; if red, the writing will be red. So we are prepared to expect that the divine message which comes through a man will come in human form—in the words of that man. And these words will vary from one writer to another, so that the same message comes now in one set of words, now in another. This is most obvious in the Gospels, where two or three evangelists set out to tell us of the same incident in Christ's life, but tell it each in his own way and his own words. As the blackboard writing is coloured by the colour of the chalk, not of the teacher, so the inspired message will be bounded by the limitations of the human author. God, in inspiring a man to write, does not give him a particular literary style, and if the man spells badly before being inspired, he will continue to spell badly. If his command of language is faltering and his literary style poor, then the divine message comes to us in blunt and simple words, with no eloquent and rounded phrases—as it has, for example, in St Mark's Gospel.

However, every comparison limps, and eventually stops short. And our comparison between the inspired writer and the piece of chalk breaks down at this point, because while the chalk is a passive, inanimate instrument, doing only what it is made to do, the inspired writer is a man, a thinking being with free will, living in a particular place and at a particular point in history, a man with his own special talents, tastes and temperament. His free will and all his dignity as an independent rational being remain untrammelled under the influence of inspiration, just as they do under the influence of grace. For inspiration really is a grace given to a man for a specific purpose—the writing of a book which contains God's word. Inspiration does not make the writer less human—or more learned. It does not carry him into a new age and environment, nor transplant him to a new culture. Each of the inspired writers remains a child of his age and upbringing, and while all through the Bible the message is God's, the words are those of Jeremiah, of Isaiah, of Luke, of Paul.

That is why the voice of God comes to us in the Bible with such a variety of human accents. Ecclesiastes looks at life around him and writes in a tone of bleak pessimism and disillusionment: "For of the wise man as of the fool there is no enduring remembrance, seeing that in the days to come all will have been long forgotten. How the wise man dies just like the fool! So I hated life, because what is done under the sun was grievous to me; for all is vanity and a striving after wind" (*Eccles.* 2:16–17).

Ecclesiasticus looks around him at the same world and writes a book which breathes contentment and satisfaction:

> ... you who fear the Lord, hope for good things,
> for everlasting joy and mercy.
> Consider the ancient generations and see:
> who ever trusted in the Lord and was put to shame?
> Or who ever persevered in the fear of the Lord and was forsaken?
> Or who ever called upon him and was overlooked?
> For the Lord is compassionate and merciful.
>
> (*Ecclus.* 2:9–11).

Jeremiah is excitable and dramatic, while his contemporary, Ezekiel, writes with calm and poise. Isaiah, the influential confidant of kings, writes stately Hebrew; Amos, the lonely shepherd of the Judean mountains, shouts rough agricultural metaphors at his audience. He addresses the ladies of Bethel: "Hear this word, you cows of Bashan" (*Amos* 4:1). St Paul dictated letters to his young communities at high speed, and the words and ideas tumble out so rapidly that we gasp for breath as we try to keep pace. The author of 2 Maccabees, on the other hand, finds writing a painful process, and says so: "For us who have undertaken the toil of abbreviating, it is no light matter, but calls for sweat and loss of sleep" (2:27). And at the end of his task he is by no means satisfied with the result, and the Old Testament concludes with his apologies, and shrewd excuse. Read them in 2 Maccabees 15:38–39. Quite clearly, not all the inspired writers wrote with equal facility. And only their common inspiration allows us to include the clumsy repetitions of the Books of Chronicles in the same book as the serene meditations of St John.

We are now in a position to eliminate a false notion of inspiration that was current for a time. An inspired book is not one that was dictated word by word to the author by God. This is the ancient and now abandoned theory of verbal dictation. Such a procedure, of course, would make the author a merely passive instrument, just like the piece of chalk, and would not allow him the use of his reason. He would be merely the record-player of the holy Spirit. This is an insult to rational man that God would never be guilty of. Besides, this would make inspiration a miraculous intervention of God, and we understand inspiration to be a grace from God, not a miracle. God does not write the book *for* the human author; he writes it *through* the human author.

The writer, then, is neither obliterated nor paralysed by the gift of divine inspiration, but he is enabled to do what he could never have done alone—to convey God's message to men "in apt words and with infallible truth".

Book

What kind of book results from this unique co-operation of God and a man in a literary enterprise? Because God is its author it will speak of him with authority, and will point the way to him with no shadow of error. And because man is its author it will have the appearance, structure and characteristics of any written document. The facts it contains may have been gathered slowly and carefully, as any historian collects his material. The author of 2 Maccabees tells us that he got his facts by summarizing five existing (non-inspired) books written by one Jason of Cyrene (2 *Macc.* 2:23).

Inspired books will use all the normal human means of communicating ideas in language, and thus the Bible contains strictly historical writing, poetry, parables, metaphors, drama. And no section of the Bible is written like a modern textbook, with general principles in heavy type, followed by a tabulated list of explanations and proofs. This is our twentieth-century and Western way of teaching—but the books of the Bible are neither twentieth-century nor Western. We must not expect them to do what they never set out to do.

Inerrancy

This is an important point to remember when we speak about one of the results of inspiration, namely, the inerrancy of the Bible. Since God is the principal author of the Bible, the Bible is

God's word, and God's word must be true—it can contain neither error nor inner contradiction. Its truth, however, is expressed in human words and channelled through human habits of thought. Therefore, to find the divine message in any part of the Bible we must read the words in their full human context, by taking account of the author, the age in which he lived, and his way of thinking and writing. The biblical authors *thought* like men of their time, and if the men of their time thought the earth was flat, then the inspired author will think this also. It is not a condition of inspiration that God should supply him with a twentieth-century textbook of geography. The biblical authors *wrote* like men of their time, and a knowledge of their idiom of thought and speech is the only way to understand what they say. After all, we have to understand our contemporary idiom in order to avoid grave confusion. A few examples may help.

When somebody is called (regrettably) an ass, we don't naively suppose that he has grown long ears; we make all the necessary mental adjustments (automatically and often unconsciously) to arrive at the meaning intended by the speaker. When the Bible uses a similar figure of speech we easily recognize it as a figure of speech, for example when John the Baptist points out Christ as the "lamb of God", or Christ refers to Herod: "Go, tell that fox . . ." Again, in our contemporary literature we acknowledge a type of writing known as fiction. We may be intensely moved by a work of fiction, but even then we don't accept it as an historical record. People have been known to weep at a film, to be moved to hot anger by a book—while all the time aware that film and novel were works of fiction. Similarly, we do not demand historical verification of biblical fiction, when we recognize it. We don't ask the name of the man who went down from Jerusalem to Jericho, nor the address of the inn to which the Good Samaritan brought him. The Bible says that these things happened, but we must not accuse it of error when we realize that the story is a piece of imagination.

Again, in reading any passage of the Bible, we need to be aware of its literary context—when, by whom, to whom, and in what circumstances a phrase is said or an action is done. We all know how easily words can betray us, even words that we use every day. In our ordinary speech we are accustomed to look for the context in order to determine the exact meaning of many words and phrases. It is impossible to resist the temptation to borrow a couple of delightful examples from Fr Alexander Jones. If a boy tells you: My Daddy has a new vice—it is wise to inquire if his father is a carpenter or mechanic before rushing to strange conclusions. And only the context in which we find it will determine the meaning of the phrase "Beat it". If we hear it said by a bigger boy to a smaller boy in the school yard—the little boy probably moves away. But if we read it in a cookery book, the meaning is quite different. The moral is: since this recourse to context is necessary in the language we are so familiar with and in the circumstances of our daily lives, how much more necessary is it in reading a translation of an ancient book, written in far other circumstances and in a much more primitive language. These are all elementary rules, but we must accustom ourselves to using them in our Bible reading in order to find the truth of the inspired books.

Finally, do we sometimes feel that sections of the Old Testament are unedifying? Do we feel surprised that Abraham could have a concubine, or consider that the Susanna story of Daniel 13 is somehow unworthy of an inspired book? If so, it indicates that we need to read the Bible much more than we do. Because God was not ashamed to come down to the level of people like these. And we have already heard Paul tell Timothy: "*All* scripture is inspired by God and profitable for teaching, for reproof, for correction . . ." The Bible is a very honest book, and it speaks of man as he is, not as we would like him to be. We must learn to see the great characters of the Bible as it sees them—as men of the rough milieu of the ancient Near East, not as haloed figures in a stained-glass masterpiece. With all their crudity and frailty, they were chosen to be God's friends and to carry the torch of faith through the world. David danced with joy before the Ark of the Covenant, but then fell into adultery—and arranged for it by murder. Simon Peter was a threefold traitor—but still the Prince of the Apostles. As Fr Hubert Richards puts it: Peter "had so much faith that he jumped into the sea, and so little faith that he went under." As we read the Bible more, we shall have little difficulty in recognizing our brothers in its pages.

In short, the Bible is the word of God and the words of men, and it talks about God as he is, and about men as they are. In writing it, the authors were aided by divine inspiration, but they still had to use reason and talents and energy. In reading it, we are expected to use our reason and talents and energy, and to pray for light to find and understand the word of God beneath the words of men.

We can learn much about the nature of inspiration by turning over in our minds the points of comparison between two divine gifts that are by no means unrelated: the *word* of God and the *Word* of God, the inspired word and the incarnate Word. Christ is the Word of God in human nature; the Bible is the word of God in human language. At the incarnation Mary is over-shadowed by the power of the Most High; in inspiration the writer is overshadowed by the Spirit of God. Christ has divine and human parentage—God and Mary; the Bible has divine and human authors—God and inspired men. God made use of Mary's human nature to bring forth the Word-made-flesh; similarly, God makes use of the author's human talents to create an inspired book. The incarnation centres around three persons— God, Mary and Christ; inspiration involves three elements— God, a human writer and a book. Christ is truly God and truly man—fully divine and fully human; the Bible is fully the word of God and fully the word of man. Christ did not become a man of indeterminate place and time—he became a Jew of the first century; an inspired book is not a kind of universal and anony-mous document—it comes from a specific century and a specific country. Finally, just as the incarnate Word is "one who in every respect has been tempted as we are, yet without sinning" (*Heb.* 4:15), so the inspired word of God is like human language in every way, error alone excepted. No wonder that some of the early Christian writers spoke of two incarnations of God's Word, one in human nature, the other in human language.

CHAPTER 2

Our Father Abraham

Reading: Genesis, chapters 12–25
Ecclesiasticus, chapter 44

SINCE childhood days our minds are peopled by a host of shadowy figures. Occasionally we are reminded of them for an instant, and then allow them to drift back again into the shadows of the subconscious. They are a mixed lot—Peter Pan, William Tell, Methuselah, Helen of Troy, Rip van Winkle . . . Is Abraham among them? Is he merely one of those darksome characters, almost unknown quantities, that lurk in the underworld of our minds? For many, perhaps he is. So it is necessary to focus the searchlight of historical fact and modern knowledge on the person of Abraham, because he is much too important to be left in the shadows.

Abraham, the man and his times, form the obvious and ideal starting-point for any serious attempt to understand the Old Testament. The Old Testament is our salvation story, the story of the long preparation of mankind for the great act of God that took place on Good Friday. And at the beginning of that slow process stands the giant figure of Abraham.

Again, Abraham is the ideal starting-point to the Old Testament story because he was the first to be called by God—and called into the country that was to be the homeland of Christ. He was the first to be given that strange and startling command: "walk before me, and be blameless" (*Gen.* 17:1). He was the first to hear God promise a golden future to man: "And I will give to you and to your descendants after you, the land of your sojournings,

all the land of Canaan, for an everlasting possession; and I will
be their God" (*Gen.* 17:8). And right through history to the birth
of Christ these promises never left the family of Abraham, until
they were fulfilled in the Messiah and his kingdom.

No wonder, then, that Old Testament and New combine to
sing the praises of Abraham and point to him as a father. In
Isaiah 41:8 God calls him "Abraham, my friend". Isaiah 51:1-2
advises all Israelites:

> . . . look to the rock from which you were hewn,
> and to the quarry from which you were digged.
> Look to Abraham your father
> and to Sarah who bore you;
> for when he was but one I called him,
> and I blessed him and made him many.

Christ, in speaking to the Jews, refers to him as "your father
Abraham" (*John* 8:56). But he is not merely the father of the
Jews; in Romans 4:16 Paul writes of "those who share the faith
of Abraham, for he is the father of us all". And Hebrews 11:8–19
is a charming summary of Abraham's life that deserves to be read.
The common biblical title for him is "our father Abraham"; all
through their history the Israelites looked back to him as the
source of their race. But his paternity was more than physical and
ethnic ancestry; above all else, he was the father of their faith—
the father of all believers.

Time and Place

The Abraham story is told in Genesis 12–25. The fifty chapters
of Genesis cover an incalculable span of time, and yet fourteen of
them are devoted to Abraham alone. This shows that the authors
of Genesis regarded him as the most important single figure in the
pre-Moses period. They regarded him as the greatest of the
Patriarchs, those father-figures of Israel, the first men to grapple
with the will of God and try to live it as best they understood.
Nowhere does Genesis give us dates of birth, marriage and death
for the Patriarchs, but by combining the Bible data with what we

can learn of the civilizations of the ancient Orient, we can set the Patriarchs against the background of their time, and discover something about their lives and laws and customs. Let us try to do this for the life and times of Abraham.

Genesis 11:28 identifies Abraham's birthplace as a city called "Ur of the Chaldeans". Remains of this city have been excavated, so we are sure of its position, size and importance. It is in the southern part of the Euphrates valley, in the area known as Mesopotamia; it is now the country of Iraq. It is good to keep in mind that all Old Testament history centres around three river valleys—Euphrates, Nile and Jordan. The Euphrates valley gave the world the great cultures of Babylon and Persia; the Nile saw the architectural splendour of monument, temple and palace that was ancient Egypt; and the Jordan valley was the cradle of our faith. All Old Testament history marches up and down the banks of these three rivers—and it never goes outside that area. Abraham is one of the few individuals who traversed all three in his lifetime. He was born in Ur, moved north to Haran, then emigrated south-west to Palestine, fled further south to Egypt in time of famine, and returned to wander along the uplands between the Jordan and the Mediterranean until he died. This area, stretching from the Persian Gulf to Ethiopia, is called the Fertile Crescent; it is in the shape of a crescent, and the three river valleys form an area of welcome green surrounded by the vast desert regions that appear on modern maps as Sa'udi Arabia and Iran.

When did Abraham live? We can now say with confidence that he lived in the nineteenth century B.C.—about 1850. And we can say something of the kind of world into which he was born. The nineteenth and eighteenth centuries formed an age of crisis in the Fertile Crescent. It was a time of war and invasion. The kings of Sumeria had ruled Mesopotamia for over a century, but their sun was setting. Wandering tribes from the surrounding desert had long looked with envy at the rich land and wealthy cities of the Euphrates valley, and about 1900 they began to drift in in increasing numbers. These invaders were Western Semites, and to these the family of Abraham belonged. Excavations by Sir

Leonard Woolley show the destruction of the city of Ur at this time, and into this event we can fit the information of Genesis 11:31—Abraham's father and his whole household moved out of Ur and "when they came to Haran, they settled there". The collapse of the city of Ur caused a migration of the inhabitants north to another city, and Abraham's journey was part of that population movement.

We can say the same thing about the far more significant event in Abraham's life—his call to follow the finger of God to an unknown destination. Genesis 12:1 states it thus: "Now the Lord said to Abram, 'Go from your country and your kindred and your father's house to the land that I will show you.'" This verse, perhaps, leaves us with the idea that Abraham set out alone, a solitary figure, on the 500-mile journey south into Palestine—the only moving person in a static world. But life is not like that, and the Bible narrative does not oblige us to picture him like that. Our archeological evidence clearly shows that the era of Abraham was one of many tribal movements—migrations of large groups of people in various directions. Besides, we must continually remind ourselves that Abraham was a nomad—with no fixed abode.

This is the first of four words that summarize the significance and the message of Abraham. Around these four we shall attempt to centre our few remarks. They are: nomad, faith, covenant, and election. Being a nomad, a wanderer, dictated the course of Abraham's life in human terms, and its geographical boundaries. His faith enabled him to see, even in his wandering life, a divine purpose. The covenant, or treaty, with God dominated his career, and made him an active instrument in the unfolding of God's plan, and also gave him the conviction that he was the exclusive property of God. Finally, all this happened because God elected, or chose, Abraham, not the other way about. And he chose Abraham freely; he could have chosen anybody else. God could say to Abraham, as Christ said to the Apostles: "You did not choose me, but I chose you". These four words—nomad, faith, covenant and election—are the ones that should come to our minds when we hear the name Abraham.

Nomad

Because the nomadic life is so foreign to us, so difficult to picture, it is worth lingering a little on it. To understand Abraham—and the Patriarchal era—we must try to understand what this nomadic life involved. The life of the nomad was a hard one, with material comforts reduced to the minimum. His home was his tent, and the family kept close to that tent and to one another. A man alone in the desert cannot survive. Abraham, his family and servants, formed a tight little group of about 350 people (*Gen.* 14), bound together by the ties of blood and common danger. Merely to exist on the rim of the desert was difficult. The only means of livelihood were the flocks of sheep and goats, and with them the whole clan had to move from one pasture to another. Survival in these circumstances demanded great powers of resistance, courage and composure. The law that the nomad lived by was the rough law of the desert, a justice meted out by the head of the clan, without written code, or judges, or jails. The nomad was a proud man—proud of his independence, of his sense of liberty, of the freedom that his homelessness gave him. And the nomad was often a violent man, for he lived in daily danger of attack from passing caravans and neighbouring tribes and invading armies. The nomad spent his whole life fighting for his existence and for the survival of his clan. Such a man was Abraham.

He was one of thousands of nomadic or semi-nomadic families that drove their flocks before them, going from pasture to pasture, sometimes driven onwards by famine (as happened to Abraham in Genesis 12), sometimes by hostile invaders (as described in Genesis 14), sometimes by the need to find wider pastures for a growing flock (as in Genesis 13). Thus, biblical evidence and secular research combine to give us a picture of a man and his family and his possessions—moving from place to place. And the call of Abraham means that God made use of these historic facts and circumstances to achieve his intentions through Abraham. Genesis 12:1 does not necessarily mean a dramatic revelation made to Abraham; it can mean that God used the historical fact

of a migration of people to lead Abraham out of the valley of the
Euphrates and bring him into the valley of the Jordan. But,
whether God intervened in some miraculous manner to beckon
Abraham forward on the road to salvation, or whether he used an
unspectacular nomadic movement to lead him on, the fact remains
that the call of Abraham set in motion the salvation-process in
the world. And however Abraham got the information, whether
by instant revelation or prolonged meditation, he had the conviction that, in leaving Haran and going south to Canaan, he was
obeying a divine command. He knew that he was an instrument
of God and that total obedience to this God was his duty as a
man. The call of Abraham, then, merits a closer look.

Now the Lord said to Abram, "Go from your country and your
kindred and your father's house to the land that I will show
you. And I will make of you a great nation, and I will bless you,
and make your name great, so that you will be a blessing. I will
bless those who bless you, and him who curses you I will curse;
and by you all the families of the earth will bless themselves."

(Gen. 12:1-3)

This is one of the most important texts in the Bible for the religious history of Israel and of all humanity. We notice, first of all,
that the promises are made, not to Abraham personally or his
family exclusively—they are for "all the families of the earth".
The call of Abraham is not an act of divine love meant only for
an insignificant West Semitic tribe—it is an act of divine love that
is destined to touch all men. Because from Abraham would come
the Chosen People, and from them would come Christ, and from
Christ would spring the Church, through which we are all saved.
All that is expressed here in the phrase: "by you all the families
of the earth will bless themselves".

Secondly, we notice how the text lingers on the items that
Abraham must leave behind. "Go from your country and your
kindred and your father's house." Not for him any more the
security and social life of a wealthy city; he can forget about Ur
and Haran now, and become a wanderer—"as in a foreign land,
living in tents", as Hebrews 11 puts it. In fact, there is a series

of separations in his life. He is separated from his birthplace, Ur (*Gen.* 11); from his relatives at Haran (chapter 12); finally from his nephew Lot (chapter 13). In the Old Testament the men who did God's work, who represented him before the public, were generally men separated from their fellows, men who walked a lonely road. And while promised that he would be the father of a great nation, Abraham was asked to spend a long and unsettled life among strangers. He even had to bargain with strangers for his burial place (*Gen.* 23), the only plot of land in Palestine that he could call his own.

Faith

But while Genesis 12 is very clear about what Abraham is leaving, it is very vague about his destination—"to the land that I will show you". He has to set out for an unknown country, one that he had never seen before, with only the conviction that this is the plan of God for him. Obedience, without question and without hesitation, in these circumstances is the first indication we get of the strong faith of Abraham.

When St Paul, in two of his letters, to the Romans and to the Galatians, speaks of Abraham, he speaks of him as pre-eminently a man who had faith in God. He says simply (quoting Genesis) that "Abraham believed God, and it was reckoned to him as righteousness". That means—he was thereby considered by God to be a just man. The faith that Paul speaks of is the same faith that Genesis speaks of, that is, faith in the biblical sense of the term. We understand faith now as a theological virtue which involves the acceptance of a body of truth, the assent of the mind given to divinely revealed mysteries, precisely because they come from God. But faith in the biblical sense is something wider than that—it is the act by which a man surrenders himself freely to God. It is belief in the truthfulness of God, belief that God can, and will, carry out any promises he makes. It is a dependence on God alone—a following of his intentions even though we cannot see the end of the road. This is the faith that led Abraham into a new country and a new mode of life; and even though the country was a strange one and the life a hard one, Abraham believed God and clung to him.

Covenant

Genesis 12:2-3 is a prophecy and a promise—that Abraham would grow into a great nation and be a source of blessing to all mankind. This promise or blessing is repeated again and again throughout his life, and forms the basis of the covenant between God and Abraham. "Covenant" is one of the Old Testament words that we must come to grips with in order to understand the story; e.g. this word occurs thirteen times in chapter 17 alone. It is used about 320 times in the Old Testament. A covenant is a pact or treaty between two parties, by which they exchange and accept obligations to one another. In this case, the pact is between God and Abraham, and the exchange is: Abraham and his posterity are to worship the one true God and him alone, while God promises to "make of you a great nation". This covenant is described in more detail in chapters 15 and 17. There, God renews his promises to Abraham. He guarantees that the family will become a populous nation and that they will possess the land of Palestine—not like Abraham, as strangers and itinerants, but as owners and masters. Also, the treaty is solemnized and ratified by external ceremonies, just as a modern treaty between nations is externalized by signing documents to be kept as perpetual reminders and proofs. The perpetual reminder in the case of Abraham is circumcision: "it shall be a sign of the covenant between me and you" (*Gen.* 17:11). The ceremony by which the treaty is signed is the sacrifice described in chapter 15. This is an interesting and dramatic ceremony that was practised at that time all over the Near East. Here it is good to read chapter 15, especially from verse 7 to the end. Birds and animals were taken and cut in two, the halves were laid at each side of a pathway, and the parties to the treaty walked between them. The significance of this was: if I fail to keep this treaty, may I be cut in two as these animals are. This explains the mysterious appearance described in verse 17: "a smoking fire pot and a flaming torch passed between these pieces." This was the visible sign of God himself walking between the halved animals to ratify his side of the agreement. Smoke and fire were the common "signs" of God's presence in the Old Testament (as in: *Exod.* 3—burning bush; *Exod.* 13—pillar of cloud and pillar of fire in the desert; *Exod.* 19—smoke and fire at Mount Sinai).

His Career

Consecrated, then, by his covenant with God, and fortified by his faith in God's promises, Abraham set out on a career of following the divine instructions, no matter what they demand or what form they take. They demanded a lot, and they took varied forms. His was a stormy and a wandering life. It is sufficient to mention some of the details. As soon as he arrived in Palestine he attempted to settle down in a specific area—"and pitched his tent, with Bethel on the west and Ai on the east" (*Gen.* 12:8). Famine soon drove him down into Egypt, where he had a brief moment of peace. But he was expelled from Egypt, and back again across the present Suez Canal he came into Palestine. He had his nephew Lot with him—whose wife was later to become famous in salt—and both Abraham and Lot had sheep and shepherds. Soon, a dispute broke out between their shepherds, and, to settle it peaceably, Abraham told Lot to choose the best land, and he would take what was left. He was prepared to pay this price for peace. But chapter 14 introduces an invasion of four kings who ravaged that countryside. Abraham was off their path, but Lot wasn't, and they captured him and led him away with them. "Then one who had escaped came, and told Abram the Hebrew" (*Gen.* 14:13), and poor peace-loving Abraham has to collect his able-bodied men and lead, for the first and only time in his life, a small army in pursuit. He rescued Lot, and returned home. But home to what? Home to a most delicate domestic situation. Abraham was old now, and so was his wife Sarah, and they had no children. Sarah suggests that he take to wife a slave-girl he had brought with him out of Egypt—Hagar. Then Sarah grows jealous and bitter, and Hagar has to flee into the desert for a time. Next, angels come and they say that Sarah will have a son. Sarah laughs openly and insults the visitors—and Abraham is left to worry and to wonder if they are angels and if their message can be true. It is—and finally Sarah brings forth a son, Isaac, who grows up a winsome child. One day Sarah sees him playing with Hagar's son, and she flies into a rage. She issues an ultimatum to Abraham: "Cast out this slave woman with her son; for the son of this slave woman shall not be heir with my son Isaac" (*Gen.* 21:10). The next verse tells us: "And the thing was very displeasing to Abraham on account of his son." But he wanted peace at any price, and so he casts out Hagar and her son (and his own) into the desert to die of hunger. Providence intervenes to save them. When they have gone, Abraham loves Isaac all the more, but now comes the command from God to sacrifice him—to take him and kill him brutally on a mountain-top. Abraham sets off to do it with the heaviest human heart that ever beat, and only at the last moment is Isaac spared. Then, Sarah dies—his life's companion in spite of all—Isaac marries, and Abraham drifts into old age and death.

This, in outline, is the biography of Abraham. A few items from this summary may be of particular interest.

Firstly, his affair with the slave-girl (*Gen.* 16). As with the rest of his life, we must see this incident from the point of view of the time and circumstances in which it happened. First, the date is about 1850 B.C., that is, 600 years before the promulgation of the Ten Commandments on Sinai. It is not reasonable to accuse Abraham of violating a commandment not yet promulgated. Again, we now know that, according to the custom in Babylon at the time, Abraham was in fact obliged to accept such a girl if she is offered to him by a childless wife. A group of American scholars excavated the city of Nuzu in north-east Iraq from 1925 to 1931, and found there a fascinating collection of clay tablets, the business documents of the old civilization. Among them are several marriage contracts. One of them reads: Kelimninu has been given in marriage to Shennima. If Kelimninu bears children, Shennima shall not take another wife: but if Kelimninu does not bear children, she shall acquire a woman of the land of Lullu as wife

for Shennima. Thus, Abraham and Sarah were following the
customs of the people among whom they had grown up. More
than that, Abraham had to keep in mind the divine promises. God
had promised salvation and blessing to all men, but through the
descendants of Abraham. These descendants were to be numerous
beyond counting: "And he brought him outside and said, 'Look
towards heaven, and number the stars, if you are able to number
them.' Then he said to him, 'So shall your descendants be'"
(*Gen.* 15:5). This, then, is Abraham's dilemma: he must have
children if God's promises are to be transmitted to all men. But
Sarah his wife is barren. What is he to do? Chapter 16 shows
Abraham and Sarah reaching their decision. So, instead of being
the sin of an unruly man, this was part of Abraham's life-long
search for the fulfilment of God's promise. As it happened, God
did not justify it, nor did it aid in the achievement of the promise,
because the son born of Hagar was Ishmael, destined to be an
outcast. God did fulfil his promises in his own time, through the
birth, at last, of Sarah's son, Isaac, through whom the salvation-
plan was worked out and carried forward.

Secondly comes one of the most homely scenes in the Old
Testament—Abraham pleads with God to spare the city of
Sodom (*Gen.* 18). Here is the man of faith, confident that God
loves him and listens to him. He makes bold with God—but
with realism and humility: "Behold, I have taken upon myself to
speak to the Lord, I who am but dust and ashes" (v. 27). With
increasing hopelessness he argues on, trying to strike a bargain
with God on behalf of a sinful city—where even ten good men
could not be found.

Thirdly, (*Gen.* 22) the command to sacrifice Isaac. This is
surely the supreme test of Abraham's faith, demanding total submission to the will of God. It was a blow, not merely to his
natural affection for his son, but also to all Abraham had lived for,
because now it seemed that the divine promises are to come to
naught—and by divine command. This is the climax of Abraham's
life, this is the final test: can he put to death his own child—and
the child of God's promise?

The sacrifice of a human being, so repugnant to us, would not have appeared too strange to Abraham. Human sacrifices were practised among the pagan inhabitants of Palestine, where he lived—and how was he to know that God did not require this of him? Also, we must remember that he was born in Ur. Now, among the archeological discoveries at Ur was an unbroken tomb of a king, complete with his retinue of wives, soldiers—and even dancing girls. Apparently, all were buried alive at the death of the king, so that they could continue to serve him in his after-life. And this happened some time before the destruction of Ur that had sent Abraham scurrying north to Haran. So his attitude to human sacrifice could hardly have been the same as ours.

Election

One final remark must be made. Abraham was called by God from all the men living on earth at the time. He was chosen—and *freely* chosen. Nothing in the Bible suggests that he was chosen because he was better or holier than his contemporaries. On the contrary, the whole narrative suggests that his greatness is the result of God's choice of him, not its cause. His greatness consists in his response to God's call, to God's choice; in our language, in his response to grace. And this is a consistent pattern in God's dealings with men that continues to our day. God chooses us to be Christians, to be saints, as St Paul puts it, not because we are better, but because he wishes to make us better. All our goodness is based, as Abraham's was, on God's free gift, and is God's achievement. We have to be wise enough to say, with Abraham: "I have taken upon myself to speak to the Lord, I who am but dust and ashes."

This, then, is the meaning and message of Abraham. The Genesis text deserves to be re-read many times. We have tried to sketch the kind of world into which he was born in the nineteenth century B.C.; the kind of life he led as head of a nomadic family; and the kind of religion that bound him to God. This religion was based on God's personal pact with him—and to this pact Abraham remained faithful, in spite of all. He shared the moral customs common to his age, but he followed the finger of God—

even to his willingness to sacrifice his son.

We began by saying that the New Testament calls him "our father Abraham". Now, perhaps, we see more clearly why we are his children. First, because we believe in the same one true God, and we believe, as Abraham did, that this God can do whatever he has promised. Secondly, because Abraham made possible the faith we now profess. He was the first link in the long chain of friends of God who carried the word of the Lord through history from Genesis through Christ to us. Thirdly, because he has given an example of faith that we, in easier times, can look to with admiration. He clung with a fierce confidence to a promise whose fulfilment lay far beyond his horizon, while we live in the era of fulfilment, and the blessing of Abraham has fallen upon us, as St Paul told the Galatians (3:14). In short, he is our father, because we, as members of Christ's Church, are part of that great nation that was promised to Abraham nearly 4,000 years ago. To repeat what we said earlier—from Abraham came the Israelite nation, and from among them Christ was born, and from Christ came the Church, and through the Church we find our way to God.

Small wonder, then, that Jews and Christians alike praise this simple, unfaltering servant of the Lord. Early in the recorded history of mankind he played two heroic parts, because in reality he founded both a race and a religion. And it is interesting that when, in the parable of Dives and Lazarus, Christ spoke of heaven and its joys, he described it by the phrase: in Abraham's bosom. Even in heaven, he will be "our father Abraham."

SOME IMPORTANT DATES

Obviously, many of these are only approximations. Thus, 1850 means—sometime in the nineteenth century. From the period of the Kings onward we enjoy greater accuracy.

B.C. 1850—Abraham
    1700—Jacob and his family take up residence in Egypt
    1250—Exodus from Egypt under Moses
    1210—Entry into Canaan under Joshua

Period of the Judges

B.C. 1020—Saul becomes Israel's first King
1000—David
961—Solomon
922—Partition of the Kingdom
722—End of the Northern Kingdom (Israel)
586—Fall of Jerusalem; end of the Southern Kingdom
(Juda)

The Babylonian Captivity

537—Edict of Cyrus; end of the exile

Return of the exiles to Jerusalem

515—Completion of the Second Temple
330—Palestine becomes part of the Greek Empire
167—Revolt of the Maccabees
63—Pompey captures Jerusalem; Judea becomes part of
the Roman Empire
37—Herod the Great becomes king

CHAPTER 3

Moses and the Exodus

Reading : Exodus, chapters 1–18
Psalm 114
Ecclesiasticus, chapter 45
Acts of Apostles, chapter 7

THIS chapter could be equally well entitled: Moses of the Exodus, or: Moses in the Exodus, because this is one of those occasions in history when a man and an event are inseparably bound together. It is not possible to talk of Moses without speaking of the exodus; it is not possible to discuss the exodus without involving Moses.

Moses is an example of a mediator between God and men—he spoke and acted on behalf of God before men. His words and his actions were never his alone—they were also God's. And they were never for the benefit of an individual, but for a whole people. This role of Moses has two aspects, because he was both leader and legislator. As leader, he is the key figure in the exodus; as legislator, he is the central figure in the covenant at Sinai. In this chapter we shall speak about Moses as leader: in the next we shall say something about his work as legislator.

Leader

If one wished to summarize the life and work of Moses as leader of the Israelites, the phrase to use could be: he shaped the Israelites into a single united people. In Egypt Moses found a collection of disgruntled slaves, but before his death he had welded them into the people of God. This is his greatness and the measure of his achievement. This task involved Moses in a long and thankless process. He was a leader from every point of view. He was the Hebrews' moral leader and spokesman before Pharaoh and the court of Egypt. He was their leader and guide in the desert wanderings. He was their military leader in their first skirmishes on the southern frontiers of Palestine. He was their political leader in organizing the social structure of the new racial group and in setting up the machinery for maintaining internal peace and justice. And he was a leader who was utterly dedicated to the people he led and loved. He was willing to offer his life for the people who followed him. The Book of Exodus, in chapter 32, presents a touching scene in which Moses intercedes for the people, when God wished to destroy them because of their idolatry. Exodus 32 is the story of the adoration of the golden calf, right at the foot of Mount Sinai, and immediately after they had received the Ten Commandments. Moses begs God to forgive them: "Alas, this people have sinned a great sin; they have made for themselves gods of gold. But now, if thou wilt forgive their sin—and if not, blot me, I pray thee, out of thy book which thou hast written" (v. 31-32).

To put it briefly, Moses is the instrument that God used to make the descendants of Abraham, not alone a unified people, but God's own people. The life and activity of Moses is really God's call and choice of Israel to be the people of God. And it is interesting to see the parallel between the experience of Abraham, as we outlined it in the last chapter, and the experience of Israel under the leadership of Moses. We saw that God's call to Abraham was gratuitous, a free act of divine love owing nothing to human merits. Similarly, God's choice of Israel is free, and owes nothing to the character of this fickle and stubborn race. Secondly, God took Abraham out of his birthplace and way of life, detached him from family and friends. In the exodus, God takes Israel out of Egypt, uprooting these Hebrews from the existence they had known. Again, God led Abraham through a long and turbulent nomadic life. And in the exodus God launched the Israelites on a strange and wandering adventure, whose destination was God's choice and whose duration was God's decision.

Finally, God made a covenant with Abraham, and allowed him-self to be called by the Old Testament "the God of Abraham". We shall see that, through Moses, God makes a covenant with Israel at Mount Sinai, and will become known henceforth as "the God of Israel".

You see the resemblances and the differences. God's method is the same in both cases, but, whereas Abraham was a tribal chieftain, leading his family after him, Moses is the leader of a whole nation, and carries the weight of God's people on his shoulders.

Still, side-by-side with the greatness of his character and the immensity of his task, Moses was a man among his fellow-men, a man of his particular time, circumstances and civilization. And we cannot hope to understand the man unless we have some knowledge of his place and time in the human caravan.

Egypt in the Thirteenth Century B.C.

The life-span of Moses fits somewhere into the thirteenth century B.C., and it is spent entirely in the areas that we call to-day Egypt and the Sinai Peninsula. The Egypt into which he was born had long passed the apex of its glory—the great Pyramids were already standing in the desert plain beyond the Nile, and the complicated Egyptian picture-language was already old. It was still a great and wealthy empire, and the valley of the Nile was a green and fertile region that produced abundant crops and fat cattle, even in those periods when the rest of the Near East was arid and semi-barren.

It was the fertility of the Nile that first brought the Hebrews into contact with Egypt. We have already seen that, 600 years before the time of Moses, Abraham had been driven south to Egypt by famine in Palestine. From this time onward, Egypt remained, in the eyes of the Hebrews, the land of corn. Then Genesis 42 shows the patriarch Jacob sending his sons down to Egypt to buy wheat, because Palestine was once more gripped by famine. Famine came often to Palestine, because crops often failed, due to inadequate rainfall, stony soil and noxious insects. Jacob's

son, Joseph, had risen to prominence in Egypt, and the Book of
Genesis ends with a happy reunion of the old man Jacob and all
his sons in the land of Goshen, a part of northern Egypt. There
they lived for roughly 400 years, generation after generation of
the descendants of Abraham, and grew prosperous and fat, until:
"there arose a new king over Egypt, who did not know Joseph"
(*Exod.* 1:8). Probably there was a succession of kings who had no
respect for the memory of Joseph, or the dignity of the Hebrews.

We may take it that the events described in the opening chapters of Exodus took place during the long reign of Rameses II
—from 1290 to 1224. This Pharaoh, who continued to despise
Joseph's descendants in the land of Goshen, became famous for
his construction projects, especially in the area of the Nile delta,
beside the land of Goshen. Naturally, his ambitious building
schemes demanded a large supply of cheap labour, and equally
naturally he drew this supply from the despised Hebrews. This
is the sad state of affairs described in Exodus 1:13-14. "So they
made the people of Israel serve with rigour, and made their lives
bitter with hard service, in mortar and brick, and in all kinds of
work in the field; in all their work they made them serve with
rigour."

Rameses' contempt for the Hebrews turned into hatred and
fear, because their numbers continued to increase, and they
formed a potentially dangerous pocket of foreigners living on
Egyptian soil. So he devised a scheme to ensure their ultimate
eradication: he instructed the Hebrew midwives: "When you
serve as midwife to the Hebrew women, and see them upon the
birthstool, if it is a son, you shall kill him; but if it is a daughter,
she shall live."

This was not successful; the midwives could not, or would not,
obey him. Therefore he issued an imperial edict to all his subjects:
"Every son that is born to the Hebrews you shall cast into the
Nile, but you shall let every daughter live." At this critical
moment, enter Moses—and the story of the Book of Exodus picks
up momentum. Moses continues to be the central figure in all that
follows in the Bible until we come to the end of the Pentateuch, as
the first five books of the Old Testament are called. He dominates

Exodus, Leviticus, Numbers and Deuteronomy: Exodus chiefly as leader, and the other books as legislator. But our immediate concern is with the first eighteen chapters of the Book of Exodus.

An easy way to become familiar with the outlines of the life of Moses is to read the good short summary of it found in Acts 7:20–44, part of St Stephen's "speech from the dock". The life of Moses falls into three periods:

1. Up to his flight into the desert of Midian—his birth, education, first contact with his own people, his flight from justice.
2. Up to the exodus—his years in Midian, his marriage, his call by God, the miracles before Pharaoh.
3. His years in the desert with the Israelites.

It may strike you immediately that there is here a strong resemblance to the familiar three-fold division of Christ's life into infancy, hidden life and public ministry.

Birth and Youth

About this first period of his life there is little that need be said. The story is told in the second chapter of Exodus. The helpless baby floating on the Nile in a basket made of reeds has always made an appealing picture. Again, as we pass by, please spare a glance for the resemblance to the story of the birth of Christ: both children's lives are threatened—and by a cruel king; both are hidden for a time—and in Egypt. The consequence of the adverse circumstances of his birth is that Moses is removed from his own people and reared and educated at the court of the Pharaoh. The word "Pharaoh", incidentally, is a Western pronunciation of two Egyptian words—per 'a—meaning "big house". The word is used, then, in the same sense as we use "the White House", or "10 Downing Street". One result of this education is that Moses is given an Egyptian name; one of the many ironies of history, sacred and secular, is that Israel's greatest leader should bear a foreign name. Moshes=the one born, and it comes from the same word as the name of the Pharaoh, Rameses. Rameses=Ra-moshes, meaning: born of the god Ra. Another and more important result is that Moses received a superior education; as St Stephen puts it (*Acts* 7:22): "Moses was instructed in all the wisdom of the Egyptians." Besides the manners of the court, this wisdom included the mathematical knowledge for which the Egyptians were then famous, and the skill in design and architecture that was the glory of ancient Egypt. Surely all this would later give him a status in the eyes of his more ignorant fellow-Israelites, and it was a providential preparation for the work he was later to supervise—the construction of the Tabernacle and the Ark of the Covenant, the measurements and design of which are described in such detail in Exodus 25–30.

It is against such a background, then, that we see Moses walking out to establish the first conscious contact with his persecuted people. No words could improve on the biblical version of the encounter, and you should promptly read it in Exodus 2:11–15.

In the Desert

Here begins the second section in the life of Moses—his period in the land of Midian (or Madian). This territory is away to the east of Egypt, and on our maps it appears as a corner of Sa'udi Arabia. There Moses marries, has children, and settles down to the life of a humble nomadic shepherd tending the flocks of his father-in-law. So Moses, brought up in the luxury, lust and laziness of the Egyptian court, now leads the life of a poor, hardworking shepherd. This primitive existence, close to nature and in the silence of the desert, was a preparation of the spirit for the great function he was to fulfil in the salvation story. Just as the first period of his life was a providential preparation in the material elements, so this second period was a providential preparation in the spiritual elements. Because here, in the desert of Midian, Moses found God.

This is the story that is told in Exodus 3–4. There it is put in the form of a miraculous appearance of God to Moses—an appearance in the shape of a bush that burned but was not consumed, and in the form of a long dialogue between God and

Moses. It is a revelation of God to Moses—a revelation that is the climax and culmination of a gradual and profound spiritual experience. The years in the desert were years of pondering and wondering for Moses—and finally he came to know and to accept the one true God. We do not know what type of religious ideas Moses brought with him into the desert, but we must, to be realistic, presume that at the court of Pharaoh he had been taught the Egyptian religious ideas of the day—and these included sun-worship and ancestor-worship. But whatever ideas he began with, Exodus 3–4 demonstrate that the desert interlude was his quest for God, a quest that ended successfully. At Mount Horeb, which is the same as Mount Sinai, Moses re-discovered the God of his fathers. This is the idea of the desert that later Jewish religion retained; they continued to regard the desert as a kind of novitiate, a place where one could come face-to-face with God. Thus we find the whole people of Israel in the desert before their entry into the Promised Land. John the Baptist hid himself in the desert before he came to the Jordan to point out God to men. Christ himself retired to the desert before launching his public ministry. St Paul tells the Galatians that he "went away into Arabia" (1:17) before he began his preaching career as an apostle. And, of course, for Moses, we can also see how the period in Midian was another providential preparation—a practical apprenticeship for the task of leading the Israelites through a trackless desert that they had never seen. Moses was familiar with at least some of it.

Encounter with God

The third and fourth chapters of Exodus deserve to be read many times, and read slowly. This appearance of God in the form of a burning bush, and this conversation of God with Moses, is the Bible's way of describing the call or vocation of Moses. The dialogue here spells out the convictions and resolutions with which Moses returned from his desert novitiate. These convictions included: the holiness of God, God's personal care for Israel, God's omnipotence, and the conviction that he himself will be guided to act and speak for God. The call that comes to this rough shepherd of Midian is no small or easy one: "Come, I will send you to Pharaoh that you may bring forth my people, the sons of Israel, out of Egypt" (*Exod.* 3:10).

Quite naturally, Moses objects: "Who am I that I should go to Pharaoh . . ?" (v. 11). God retorts: "But I will be with you . . ." (v. 12). But Moses is still aware that he is an unknown quantity to his fellow-Hebrews, and so he asks God his name! If he is to go to them as an ambassador, whose ambassador shall he proclaim himself?

God's reply was: "I am Yahweh" (v. 14). This is a word over which scholars and theologians have puzzled ever since, and gallons of ink have flowed in the attempt to understand it fully. It is enough to say here that the word is a part of the Hebrew verb "to be", and that the phrase "I am Yahweh" is normally translated as I am Who am, or I am Who I am. But what ideas did this word Yahweh bring to the minds of the Israelites? Probably this: Yahweh is the God who not alone always is, but always is present and near. For them, "to be" often meant "to be present". Thus, the name Yahweh is a statement and a guarantee of God's continual presence to them. This meaning of the word may be confirmed by verse 12: "But I will be with you." This name the Israelites adopted as their specific name for the God of Israel, and later in their history they came to treat it with such reverence that they never pronounced it aloud. In the days of the Kings, this name could be uttered aloud only by the high priest, and by him only on occasions of great liturgical solemnity. Whenever an Israelite met the word "Yahweh" in reading the Scripture text he substituted another word for it. Confusion ultimately grew up between the two words, and thus was born the mongrel word "Jehovah"—a word that exists in no language and is thus a monstrosity. We might make a firm resolution never to use the word "Jehovah". The Hebrew word is Yahweh, and in our English Bibles Yahweh is generally translated as "the Lord."

Armed with this new name for God, and with God's commission to rescue the Israelites from their pitiful condition of slavery, and with his brother Aaron to help him, Moses returns to Egypt to begin what we might call his public ministry. And at last we are ready to speak about the plagues and the exodus. Perhaps this introduction has been too long. But it is important for us to understand that Moses did not drop suddenly down from heaven, a dynamic and imposing figure, confound the Pharaoh by a series of sensational miracles, and march proudly out the desert road at the head of an admiring throng. It is important for us to see that Moses was a man like other men, and that a long preparation was necessary before he was fit to undertake the mission God had destined for him. This early section of the life of Moses is passed over in silence in most books, and this is a pity. We know Moses better, and we see the workings of God's providence better, when we realize that even a man of the gigantic stature of Moses needs to come to grips with himself and with God. Knowledge of himself—of his quick temper, of his fear—drove Moses out of Egypt into the desert; knowledge of God and of his love for Israel brought Moses back into Egypt to be the leader and liberator of his people. If we omit this first part of his life, we may come to know something about the exodus, but we shall never know much about Moses. And, after all, the man is always more important than the incident.

The Ten Plagues

The fifth chapter of Exodus opens abruptly with the scene: Moses before Pharaoh. The result of the royal audience was disastrous. (At this point, read *Exod.* 5:1–14). The Hebrews shout bitterly at Moses: "The Lord look upon you and judge, because you have made us offensive in the sight of Pharaoh and his servants, and have put a sword in their hand to kill us" (v. 21). As Mgr Knox translates it: "You have made our name stink in the nostrils of Pharaoh." The glorious mission of Moses is off to a bad start; he is rejected by both parties, by Pharaoh and by his own people. So often this will be the fate of the prophets of Israel; for example, Elijah had to flee to the wilderness, Jeremiah was reviled and imprisoned.

Chapters 7–12 give us, with much repetition and in unnecessary detail, the list of ten plagues. The text follows much the same

order in dealing with each one: (*a*) the Lord sends Moses to
Pharaoh to request permission to leave, and threatens a pestilence
if he refuses; (*b*) Pharaoh does refuse, and the pestilence comes;
(*c*) Pharaoh relents, and the plague is lifted; (*d*) Pharaoh then
refuses to allow them to go—and the cycle begins again.

There is an obvious crescendo movement in the text. If we
write down the plagues in the order given in Exodus we see this
upward movement easily.

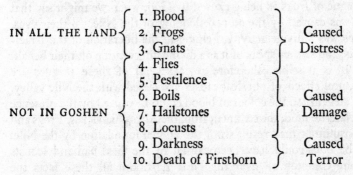

IN ALL THE LAND	1. Blood	
	2. Frogs	Caused
	3. Gnats	Distress
	4. Flies	
	5. Pestilence	
	6. Boils	Caused
NOT IN GOSHEN	7. Hailstones	Damage
	8. Locusts	
	9. Darkness	Caused
	10. Death of Firstborn	Terror

It is clear enough that the author wishes to build his story
towards a climax—the tenth plague and the exodus. And he
arranges many of the details of text and presentation to achieve
this purpose. This is probably the reason for introducing the
magicians of Pharaoh, and showing them as successful in the first
two plagues. Their success at the beginning is a device to under-
line their helplessness later on, and therefore their clear inferiority
to the power at work through Moses, and this is the point towards
which the author was aiming.

Now, we must face the question: what are we to make of this
strange series of miracles? Could such miracles have taken place?
Of course they could have. We can set no limits to the power of
God. But at the same time we must be aware that, as far as our
observation of things goes, God seems to be rather sparing in the
use of miracles. We must try to see the subject from the viewpoint
of the Old Testament writers.

They had a looser concept of miracle than we have. For them,
God used men and nature to achieve his will; God sent the proph-

ets and God sent the rain. They attributed every natural result directly to God, without mentioning any intermediary cause. For example, a modern textbook of geography will say that rain is caused by a variety of physical factors, involving condensation, moisture, clouds, temperature. Old Testament writers say simply —rain is caused by God. "... for the Lord God had not caused it to rain upon the earth" (*Gen.* 2:5). The two statements seem to be conflicting—but both are true. Similarly here, they speak of a plague of frogs as being caused by God, when we might say that it was caused by the annual flooding of the Nile. In their eyes, this was a divine activity, helping in the liberation of the Israelites, and so they speak of it as a divine intervention on their behalf.

It is possible, therefore, that several of these plagues are natural effects of physical causes associated with the Nile valley. Water turned the colour of blood could be caused by the presence of laterite mud, the sediment from the Abyssinian lakes. Frogs and mosquitoes may result from the annual inundation by the Nile. The boils could have been caused by the flies; hail and locusts were common all over the Near East. But all these facts the authors of Exodus attributed directly to Yahweh, because they saw Yahweh making use of nature as well as of Moses to achieve his purpose.

Modern thought distinguishes clearly between the "miraculous" and the "marvellous" or the extraordinary. An eclipse of the sun is extraordinary in relation to its normal shining, but it is not miraculous, because it follows from known laws of nature. The Israelites had no such distinction between the miraculous and the marvellous; they called them all "signs and wonders which Yahweh did". They were *wonders* because God did them for the Israelites, and they continued all through their history to be wonderful acts in their eyes. And they were *signs* of God's love for Israel. Everything that happened, happened because God caused it—and in this they were not wrong. Everything that God did for Israel was wonderful and a sign of his love—and in this also they were correct.

Therefore this story of the plagues is not a fairytale, not a work of unaided imagination. We must take it seriously. But we must also take it critically. That means that we must not look upon it as a photographic record of a series of events, because it does not pretend to be that. It is the account of a series of calamities that made the Israelites' departure from Egypt possible. Whether these calamities were natural or entirely miraculous, their ultimate cause was God. And to the Israelite mind they demonstrated that God was present and active in their midst. And was not this the very name he gave himself?

It is important to grasp this clearly. We are not removing the miraculous from the exodus. To say that the plagues are miracles is a perfectly satisfactory explanation. We are merely suggesting that there may be another explanation. We have no desire to eliminate the miraculous from the account of the exodus. In fact, it is not possible to do so. Apart from the death of the firstborn, for which it is difficult to suggest a natural cause, only the power of God can account for many of the items in the biblical narrative. Such items are: the sudden appearance and disappearance of the plagues, their intensity, and the exemption of the Israelites from some of them. In the end, whatever men may try to make of these events, they will always have to admit, at the very least, what has been called "the miracle of coincidence", namely, that man and nature combine at a strategic moment to achieve whatever is necessary for the forwarding of the salvation plan in the world by means of Israel.

Going Out of Egypt

Now, all that remains is the exodus itself, the act of going out of Egypt. Whether they knew it or not, the Hebrews were going out never to return. Their descendants would taste the bitterness of exile—in Assyria, in Babylon, but never in Egypt. They were leaving the valley of the Nile—and forever.

But the task of Moses was only beginning. This is where the third and final section of his life commences. Now he has to gather the Hebrews together, get them into some kind of marching order, help them to organize their goods and their flocks. This must have been a herculean task, because they had never before acted as a unit—they had no cohesion, no discipline. They are individualist and self-willed, and many times during the long march to Palestine Moses will complain bitterly of their disobedience and their stubbornness. In fact, the favourite adjective that the Bible uses of the Israelites is "stiff-necked"—an uncomplimentary one taken from the oxen under the plough that will not respond to the reins. Fifteen times that adjective is used of them, and the story shows that they richly deserve it.

How Moses led them out from Egypt into the uncharted wilderness of the Sinai Peninsula is described in part of Exodus 12 (31–41), part of chapter 13 (17–22), and in chapters 14 and 15. The story is familiar, and we need make only a few remarks about it.

(a) How many people went out? Exodus 12:37 says "about six hundred thousand men on foot, besides women and children". To talk about the early Israelite historians' use of numbers would draw us too far off-course at this point. However, Israelites did not always use numbers merely to count, and thus they are not always mathematically correct. Those who are statistically minded will have little hesitation in saying that the number 600,000 is impossible. Because 600,000 active men should mean a total of over two millions. Exodus 1:5, as well as Genesis, informs us that roughly seventy Hebrews, the family of Jacob, went into Egypt about 400 years previously. Now, following normal population laws, seventy people in 400 years would grow to about 10,000. Besides, two-and-a-half million people, marching four deep, would form a column extending over a distance of 350 miles!

(b) The route they followed? The text does not give us enough information to retrace it accurately. Some of the place-names given cannot be identified with certainty today. Most Bibles and books on the subject give a map showing an approximate route. The name "Red Sea" is unfortunate, as it is not the same place as the present-day Red Sea. This is a mis-translation for "Reed Sea", a marshy swampland near the southern end of the present Suez Canal. As with the plagues, the crossing of it was probably a combination of the natural and the supernatural, the natural element being low water due to hot East winds from the desert drying up the marshes, the supernatural element being the suddenness of the phenomenon and the providential synchronization with the needs of the Israelites.

(c) What of "the pillar of cloud by day and the pillar of fire by night" mentioned in Exodus 13:22? This is a familiar Hebrew way of *saying* that God was with them. But possibly these phenomena were present, as a way of *showing* that God was with them. They were further convinced of his presence by the supply of food and water with which their perilous desert journey was provided. Let's take the food as an example; chapter 16 speaks of quail and manna. Quail is a bird of the partridge breed, normally migrating across this region in the springtime. Manna consists in the dried remains of a type of insect found under tamarisk trees. Modern Bedouin Arabs still call this substance "manna". Chemical analysis of manna shows it to contain about eighty per cent sugar, and so it is highly sustaining. Therefore we can conclude that these wonders follow the same pattern as the whole miracle tradition connected with the exodus. The food in itself is natural, but it took the all-seeing eye and the all-achieving power of God to accomplish the miracle of coincidence by which the food was present at the time, and in the quantity, necessary for the survival of the Israelites.

Thus, protected by God and led by Moses the Israelites moved slowly forward across the desert in the direction of Mount Sinai, the mountain where Moses had come face-to-face with God in Exodus 3.

Exodus in the life of Israel

The exodus was the greatest single event in the history of Israel from the call of Abraham to the coming of Christ. That is why the Israelites recalled it constantly in prayer and ceremonial—in the prayer of the Psalms and the ceremonial of the Pasch. It remained the great watershed of Israelite history. It was the greatest thing God had done for them—it was his first redemption of enslaved men, to be the type of the second and greater redemption of

humanity enslaved by sin. It was the beginning of Israel as the
Chosen People, and therefore the beginning of the People of God.
In that sense, we can all look back to it as our spiritual birthday,
for we too are the People of God.

CHAPTER 4

At Mount Sinai

Reading: Exodus, chapters 19–35
Deuteronomy, chapters 5–6
Matthew, chapter 5

In the last chapter we said that Moses, as he marched at the head of the Israelites, played a two-fold part—he was leader and he was legislator. We mentioned the highlights of his career as leader; now we turn to some of his achievements as legislator.

We left Moses in the desert, somewhere between the Sea of Reeds and the mountain of Sinai, leading his ragged and unruly band of Israelites towards the holy mountain, towards Sinai, where he had found Yahweh, his God. His experience there will be reproduced for the whole people, because at Sinai the Israelites make their first corporate contact with Yahweh. We must ask the question (even though we cannot answer it with certainty): as they moved slowly across the desert, what did they know of the one true God? After all, they have been about four hundred years in Egypt, and the God of their fathers, the God of Abraham, Isaac and Jacob, must by now have become a dim and distant figure in their minds. They have hardly escaped contamination by the pagan beliefs and practices of Egypt. This suspicion is confirmed by Exodus 32—the incident of the golden calf—which shows how easily they slipped back into a form of idolatry that is certainly Egyptian. It is scarcely wise to cherish the illusion that the Israelites marched forward to Sinai with firm step, singing hymns of praise to the God they knew was waiting there to welcome them. We must accept the picture of them that the Book of Exodus presents: a motley and disgruntled group, "stiff-necked", quarrelling among themselves and rebelling against their leader, quick to forget their liberation from Egypt, reluctant to face the hazards of the desert, not knowing where they were going or why, with no unifying force to cement them together, and no strong religious allegiance to give them confidence in the unknown future. This unifying force, this religious allegiance, is precisely what the incidents at Mount Sinai will give them. That is why Sinai marks a turning-point in their history—and therefore in the whole salvation story. The meeting of God and Israel at Sinai is one of those historical moments that changed the face of the human story.

Israel meets God

At Sinai a unifying force and a religious allegiance were given them—and the two were one, because it is their common allegiance to Yahweh that really unites them into one nation. They became one people, not because they were of common stock, or would later occupy the same country, or use the same language; they became one people because they became the people of the one true God. Their allegiance to the same Yahweh was the bond which welded them into a single unit, a people. That is why, later on in their history, we shall see that whenever their faith grew cold their national unity shattered. Whenever they abandoned their God they were torn asunder by internal strife. This is the first indication we get of the fact, to be made so clear by Christ, that union with God and union with our fellow-men are facets of the same truth.

When we think of Sinai we tend to think exclusively of the Ten Commandments, or the Decalogue, from two Greek words meaning "ten words" (of Yahweh). But the Decalogue is only part of the story, because what the Hebrews encountered at Sinai was not a set of laws but God himself. The Sinai episode is much more than the promulgation of a code of law; it is really a terrifying meeting with their God. They discover him as a God who governs the whole of human life, and they accept the fact that henceforth, "for better, for worse, for richer, for poorer", they belong to him alone. Israel has become the people of God, and God has bound himself to be the God of Israel. This is the significance of Sinai as Exodus itself expresses it. "You have seen what I did to the Egyptians, and how I bore you on eagles' wings and brought you to myself. Now therefore, if you will obey my voice and keep my covenant, you shall be my own possession among all peoples; for all the earth is mine, and you shall be to me a kingdom of priests and a holy nation" (19:4–6).

Thus, to be true to the text, we must accustom ourselves to think of Sinai, not so much in terms of a code of conduct, as in terms of a covenant between a God who loves and a people who promise to respond. The covenant is the central fact; the code is an expression of the covenant.

The Text

Now let us look at the text of Exodus more closely and see for ourselves how this covenant story unfolds. The section of the Old Testament that we are chiefly concerned with here is short (*Exod.* 19–24), but these chapters contain several distinct subjects, as you see when you read through them carefully. These subjects, or items of information, have not all the same importance, or the same date of composition. This section, like all the Pentateuch, is not the work of a single author, but of a group of editors (it is the best name for them) who took several parallel accounts, stemming from different regions of Palestine and from different authors and different centuries, and combined them into one narrative. So we must first engage in a little disentangling.

The most obvious distinction that the text presents is that between factual narrative and legal prescription. Up to the end of chapter 19 we are dealing with people and what happens to them; this is historical narrative. But the twentieth chapter opens with the phrase: "And God spoke all these words, saying . . ." And there follows a long series of laws, carrying us right up to the end of chapter 23. Let's concentrate our attention on this legal section for a moment.

Only the first seventeen verses of it relate the Ten Commandments; the rest (roughly chapters 21–23), is a detailed code of laws, ritual, ethical and religious. This code contains rules for marriage, for slaves, the duties of parents and children, punishment of theft, the chief feasts of the year, etc. This section is called the Code of the Alliance. Now, this Code of the Alliance did not originate at Sinai, and does not belong to the Sinai period, the thirteenth century B.C. The proof of this is that most of these laws presume a kind of life that was impossible for some years after Sinai—a settled, sedentary mode of life, with private property, vineyards, cornfields: "When a man causes a field or vineyard to be grazed over, or lets his beast loose and it feeds in another man's field, he shall make restitution from the best in his own field and in his own vineyard" (*Exod.* 22:5).

The Code of the Alliance, then, belongs to a later stage in the Israelites' history, to the time when they have settled down in the land of Palestine as its owners.

The Code of the Alliance, therefore, must not be put on a par with the Decalogue. The two codes are different in date. They are different in style; the Decalogue is short and concise, the Code of the Alliance gives a list of practical applications stated at length. They are different in purpose, because the Decalogue is exclusively religious, whereas much of the Code of the Alliance is what we would call civil law, such as restitution for injuries to person or property, trespassing on another's rights. Finally, they are different in extent, because the Decalogue consists of general principles, capable of application always and everywhere, in city street or in desert tent, while the Code of the Alliance is a set of laws suited to a certain type of existence. Thus, the Decalogue is universal and immutable, while the rest of Israel's laws are subject to adaptation to different eras and changing circumstances.

The Covenant at Sinai

The result of this preliminary glance at the text is that, when we come to trace the order of events at Sinai in that fateful meeting between God and Israel, we shall omit the Code of the

Alliance. It belongs to a later period. We can then set down the order thus:

(a) Chapter 19: The preparation for the solemn event. They make a kind of retreat, and God shows his presence by the usual signs.

(b) Chapter 20: The Decalogue.

(c) Chapter 24: The covenant is ratified between God and the people by a solemn reading of the Decalogue and the offering of a sacrifice.

(a) Chapter 19: This underlines the importance of the event that is taking place. "Lo, I am coming to you in a thick cloud" (v. 9). For this coming of the Lord the people must prepare themselves: "Go to the people and consecrate them today and tomorrow . . . and be ready by the third day" (v. 10–11).

On the third day we find Sinai encircled by the now familiar signs of God's presence—cloud, smoke, lightning.

(b) Chapter 20: The giving of the Decalogue. We shall return to this in a moment.

(c) Chapter 24: The signing of the covenant. You remember Genesis 15 and the covenant with Abraham. Here in Exodus 24 we find a ceremony that dramatizes the idea of two parties binding themselves to a covenant. "And Moses took half of the blood and put it in basins, and half of the blood he threw against the altar . . . And Moses took the blood and threw it upon the people, and said, 'Behold the blood of the covenant which the Lord has made with you in accordance with all these words' " (v. 6; 8).

The blood of the victim is sprinkled first on the altar, representing God, and then on the people. Thus the two parties to the covenant have sealed their treaty in blood, which is why this is called the blood of the covenant, or blood of the testament. Over 1200 years later, one evening in Jerusalem, Christ will hand a chalice to his Apostles with the words: "This is my blood of the new covenant." And at that moment Old Testament gives way before New; what had been inaugurated at Sinai is brought to completion.

That, in outline, is what happened at Mount Sinai. In chapter

19 God is present by his signs; in chapter 20 he is present by his "ten words"; in chapter 24 he is present as a party to a treaty. All three point to one conclusion—that Sinai was the signing of a solemn covenant between God and Israel. That is why the sacrificial blood is called, not the blood of the commandments, but the blood of the covenant; that is why the container of the commandments will be called, not the ark of the commandments, but the ark of the covenant. Up to this, the Israelites had contact with Yahweh only through the instructions of Moses; at Sinai they meet him, and begin to see, very faintly, the outlines of his plan for them. That is why the Israelites always regarded the promises and warnings of Sinai as addressed, not only to Moses and his contemporaries, but to each succeeding generation, because this was a permanent covenant with God, and it was the Israelite nation, not any particular era of it, that was convenanted to Yahweh. As Deuteronomy 5:3 says: "Not with our fathers did the Lord make this covenant, but with us, who are all of us here alive this day."

All this helps us to see that the Ten Commandments are not an isolated piece of legislation, but are an expression of an abiding alliance which grapples men to God. In other words, the Decalogue is not so much a code of laws as a way of life.

That the Decalogue is a covenant document received remarkable confirmation in recent years with the discovery and translation of some oriental treaties from the fourteenth and fifteenth centuries, the same period as Exodus and Sinai. These are treaties made within the great Hittite Empire, treaties between a king or emperor and his subject nations. Their aim is to pledge a nation to loyalty to its king, and to exhort the nation to trust in the king's care and benevolence. These treaties all follow the same pattern:

1. A preamble in which the king identifies himself, and refers to his past favours to the subject nation;
2. A list of obligations imposed by the king on this nation;
3. A demand that a copy of the treaty be kept forever and be publicly read to the people;

4. A conclusion taking the form of a promise of blessings to the nation if it is faithful to the treaty, and curses if not.

A rapid glance at the Bible text is sufficient to show that the Sinai covenant is written down in this same pattern:

1. Introduction—"I am the Lord your God, who brought you out of the land of Egypt, out of the house of bondage" (*Exod*. 20:2).
2. Obligations—the Decalogue (*Exod*. 20:3-17).
3. Read to the people—as is done by Moses in Exodus 24; kept forever—in the Ark of the Covenant.
4. Blessings and threats—as in the formidable list in Deuteronomy 27-30.

From this striking similarity to the Hittite documents we can draw several conclusions. (*a*) The Decalogue text really does come from the thirteenth century B.C. (*b*) Moses set down the divine wishes in the normal civil law format of the orient of his day. (*c*) Moses and the Israelites regarded the Decalogue as part of a treaty with Yahweh. He is their new-found King, and they are his nation. They pledge themselves to be loyal to him and agree to trust in the continuation of the mercies he has shown them. Normally, when we think of the Ten Commandments we associate them with the word "obedience"; perhaps we should come closer to the Old Testament viewpoint if we use the word "loyalty". God demands of them at Sinai, not so much a blind and terror-stricken obedience to a decree, but rather willing loyalty to a God who has already demonstrated his love for them on the banks of the Nile, in the Sea of Reeds, and through the barren reaches of the desert. The idea of loyalty to the covenant both ensures the keeping of the Commandments and provides the motive for keeping them.

The Decalogue

Now we come to the text of the Decalogue. We are accustomed to the catechism listing of the Commandments, but we need to read the Old Testament text to see them in their original setting.

The Decalogue is found in Exodus 20:2–17, and again in Deuter-onomy 5:6–21, in both cases in a form longer than that found in the catechism. But their original form, the form that the Israelites received at Sinai, is shorter than the Exodus text. There are several reasons for saying this; we can mention two. First, the Ten Commandments were written on two slabs of stone, which the Israelites carried with them in the Ark of the Covenant all through the desert, and retained until the sack of Jerusalem by the Babylonians. The text that could be carved in Hebrew letters on two such portable slabs could not be a very long one. The second reason is one you can verify for yourself by a close reading of the text. The Decalogue is in two sections: (i) Commandments 1 to 3, dealing with man's relations to God; (ii) Commandments 4 to 10, dealing with man's relations to his fellow-men. Now, the "long" commandments, those to which additions and explana-tions are attached, are numbers 1, 3, 4 and 10, which are the first and last commandment in each of these two sections. Perhaps, then, these additions serve the purpose of capital letter and full stop in our mechanics of writing—they mark the beginning and the end of each section. Therefore it would seem that, in its original form, the Decalogue was a series of short, concise, staccato statements. This form has been preserved in command-ments 5, 6 and 7 (as we number them).

On the text of the Decalogue there is little to be said that is not already familiar, but sometimes even to translate them into twentieth-century English is enlightening.

Commandment 1—You shall have no other gods in my pres-ence. This is an extraordinary command in the orient of the thirteenth century B.C., when exuberant polytheism blossomed all around. In the history of religion this command appears as something unique, a precept unknown in other moral codes. This commandment excludes any god, or any object of worship, out-side Yahweh. Therefore the following sentence is really a part of that same command: "You shall not make yourself a graven image." That is why we include both in our first commandment. The reason for the specific mention of sculptured images is that at that time, and in the civilizations that Israel knew, images or figures of men and animals were normally made to represent a false god, with the result that the image was ultimately adored as the image of the god in visible form. So, in such an atmosphere, the temptation to idolatry was always a present and a pressing one, as Israel's later history shows. Thus verse 5 says: "you shall not bow down to them or serve them." This indicates that it was not the image as such that was forbidden, but the worship of it. They did have images, even in the Ark of the Covenant, and later on Moses made a serpent of bronze (*Num.* 21).

Commandment 2—You shall not pronounce the name of Yahweh your God unjustly, or falsely. This forbids them to profane the holiness of God. Just as the first commandment safeguards the uniqueness of God, the second commandment safeguards the sanctity of God. We mentioned already that later on the Israelites interpreted this so strictly that they did not even pronounce the name Yahweh.

Commandment 3—Remember the Sabbath day, to keep it holy. You will notice the change in form here; this does not begin, as the others do, by: You shall not . . . The reason is that this commandment does not institute the Sabbath; the Sabbath rest was already in existence, and they are being reminded to continue its observance. What is new here is that now the Sabbath is to be dedicated to Yahweh. The origin of the Sabbath is still plunged in obscurity, but the idea of one day in every seven being given over to God probably expresses the sacredness of the number seven. The explanation given in Exodus 20:11—a reference to Genesis 1—is a later addition and does not intend to give the origin of the Sabbath.

The Israelites always regarded the Sabbath rest as a serious obligation, and Exodus 31:14 says that those who violate it cease to belong to the community of believers. The Jews who emigrated all over the empire to the great commercial cities in Greek and Roman times brought the Sabbath observance with them, even though it often made them a laughing-stock to their pagan neighbours. Towards New Testament times the pharisees loaded down the third commandment with a multitude of prescriptions verging on the ridiculous. They gravely discussed such problems as: how many steps can one walk, how many letters (of the alphabet) can one write, without violating the Sabbath? Some rabbis said only two. Does untying the knot on a camel's halter break the Sabbath rest? It was from these human and unreasonable additions to a divine law that Christ freed us when he said: "The sabbath was made for man, not man for the sabbath; so the Son of man is lord even of the sabbath." (*Mark* 2:27–28)

With the fourth commandment we begin a new type of precept. Commandments 1 to 3—the attitude of man to God; commandments 4 to 10—the attitude of man to his fellow-men. The first three commandments are peculiar to Israel, and have no parallel in other religious codes, because they are an expression of this unique relationship between God and his chosen Israel. The remaining seven commandments represent the voice of conscience, and roughly similar laws are found outside of Israel. But what is new in them, and what is peculiar to the Decalogue, is the close connection they establish between duties to God and duties to fellow-men. In this way the covenant changed everything, and made, for the first time, a man's attitude to his fellow-men to be an expression of his attitude to God. While the first section of the Decalogue safeguarded the sacredness of God and his right to his creatures' worship, the second section safeguards the dignity of man and his right to certain human temporal assets. Too easily we regard the Decalogue as a number of onerous prohibitions; but it is a Bill of Human Rights as well as a list of duties. Commandments 4 to 10 form a declaration of a man's right to: the benefits of his children (4); his life (5); his wife (6); his property (7); his reputation (8); security of tenure in family and property (9 and 10). A few random remarks on these commandments as we pass rapidly by will suffice here.

Commandment 4—This established the sanctity and viability of the family unit, by commanding respect and support, moral and economic, for parents. It is worth noting that, in an atmosphere where women enjoyed few privileges, this precept puts father and mother on the same level.

Commandment 6—The Israelites accepted this literally, as forbidding adultery only, which, as they understood it, meant taking the wife of another. Hence its position in the Decalogue—between the prohibition of murder and that of stealing. Adultery they regarded as one of the acts that injured one's neighbour; they saw it as a crime against the woman's husband—a violation of his property and honour. It was this interpretation of the sixth commandment that allowed them to have a divorce law and re-marriage, as legislated for in Deuteronomy 24:1-4.

Commandment 8—Directly and primarily, it refers to giving false testimony against another. The Israelites were much given to litigation; their way of righting social wrongs was to appeal to judges, elders, some respected person or group. This was in evidence already before Sinai, as you can see by reading Exodus 18:13-27. In such circumstances the giving of false evidence could ruin a man's reputation or cause him to lose his property; the prohibition of such false evidence is the direct object of the eighth commandment.

Commandments 9 and 10—Both are expressed together in verse 17. The order followed in the enumeration is: first, the house, then its contents: wife, slaves, animals.

The Ark of the Covenant

These "ten words of Yahweh" were always accepted by Israel as her constitution, and her guarantee of divine protection. And the two slabs of stone on which Moses or his expert stone-cutters had carved the text of the Decalogue were the most sacred objects in Israel's possession. So they treated these tablets of stone with reverence, and constructed for them a suitable container, which they called the Ark of the Covenant, which means the container or box of the covenant. Chapters 25 and 37 of the Book of Exodus describe this Ark of the Covenant and how the Israelites made it. It was constructed with great care, adorned with the most precious wood, metals and craftsmanship possible to them, and treated with the respect due to the words of Yahweh. It symbolized for them the Lord who was always present with them.

Constructed at the base of Mount Sinai, the Ark was carried by the Israelites through the desert up to the plains of Moab and finally across the Jordan in the invasion of Joshua. Various sanctuaries were constructed for it, they brought it with them into battle, and finally King David brought it to Jerusalem. His son Solomon built the first great temple at Jerusalem to be a home for the Ark, and there it remained, the most sacred object in the Holy of Holies, until the destruction of the Temple at the fall of Jerusalem in 586 B.C. It too was probably destroyed: the Bible does not mention it again.

But, though the tablets of stone disappeared, the ten words of Yahweh remained, and continued to be guiding lights of Israel's life and religion. Around these ten stark and simple statements there gradually grew up a complex code of laws dealing with social justice and religious rites—priesthood, sacrifice, liturgy. These laws take up most of the books of Leviticus, Numbers and Deuteronomy. Much of this legislation dates from their settled possession of Palestine—as we said already about the Code of the Alliance. But all of it is an amplification and application of the Decalogue, and in that sense all of it is built on the foundation of law and order laid by Moses at and immediately after Sinai. Thus, later Judaism could refer to this whole code of law simply as the law of Moses. This is how Christ himself referred to it. So to Moses, leader and legislator of infant Israel, must go the final credit for the great body of Old Testament law, a law which involved the complete man and every aspect of his life, and which enabled him to live at peace with his God, with his fellow-men and with himself.

The Decalogue in the New Testament

We cannot leave Moses and the Decalogue without a brief glance at the terminus to which Moses and the Decalogue led humanity. We have said that the old covenant gave way to a new covenant sealed, not in the blood of an animal, but in the blood of Christ. Since the Decalogue was the expression of the old covenant, should there not be a new decalogue as an expression of the new Christian covenant of grace? No; Christ did not come to bring new laws, but he did make the old laws new. He did not abolish the Decalogue, but he perfected it. And that is what he meant when he said: "I have not come to abolish them but to fulfil them", that is to bring them to completion and perfection.

See how, for example, in the sermon on the mount, he brings the fifth commandment to completion, by extending its obligations beyond the letter of the law to the spirit of love. "You have heard that it was said to the men of old, 'You shall not kill; and whoever kills shall be liable to judgment.' But I say to you . . ." (*Matt*. 5:21–22).

What he said to them was—whoever rages in anger against his fellow-man, or treats him with contempt, or calls him a fool, this man breaks the fifth commandment. Therefore this is not simply a prohibition of murder—it is a command to love. He goes on to say that no man should go to the temple to offer sacrifice until he has first made peace with his brother. Similarly, Christ rejected their limited interpretation of the sixth commandment. It is not only the adulterer who violates this, but "every one who looks at a woman lustfully" (*Matt*. 5:28). He sweeps away the Old Testament possibility of divorce and restores marriage to its original divine constitution—a man shall cleave to his wife. And, after all, "You shall not covet your neighbour's house" is the first step towards "Blessed are the poor". The Old Testament attached to the Decalogue motives and promises, such as "Honour your father and your mother, *that* your days may be long in the land which the Lord your God gives you" (*Exod*. 20:12). In the new covenant Christ transforms motive and promise. St John puts the whole Decalogue in its proper Christian perspective in a single verse (14:23): "If a man loves me, he will keep my word, and my Father will love him, and we will come to him and make our home with him." Here we have all things made new—a new and higher motive, a new and nobler promise.

In this way, the process begun by Moses was crowned by Christ. It is not surprising that Moses appeared beside him transfigured on a hillside in Galilee. And this gives us a glimpse of how the salvation plan was gradually unfolded. Creation made men God's creatures; the covenant made them God's partners; Christ made them God's children. We are more than creatures, more than servants, more than partners; we are sons of God. This is what the coming of Christ has done for the world.

CHAPTER 5

The Paschal Lamb

Reading: Exodus, chapter 12
Joshua, chapter 5
2 Kings, chapter 23
2 Chronicles, chapter 30
Ezra, chapter 6
Luke, chapter 22

THE term "Pasch" is familiar to us since school days—it is not a new one to which we need an introduction. The aim in this chapter, then, is merely to sharpen our ideas about the Pasch, and to provide a clear mental picture that we can associate with the word. Or, rather, with the words, because our English Bibles use two words: Pasch and Passover. "Pasch" is taken from an ancient Hebrew word, and the translation "Passover" is explained in Exodus 12:26–27. "And when your children say to you, 'What do you mean by this service?' you shall say, 'It is the sacrifice of the Lord's passover, for he passed over the houses of the people of Israel in Egypt, when he slew the Egyptians but spared our houses.'"

Now, the Pasch is only one of several annual religious ceremonies in the Old Testament calendar, and you may wonder why we devote a chapter to it—and at this point. Well, there are several reasons; the following are some of them.

(*a*) Since the Pasch was a sacrifice, it gives us an opportunity of taking a look at sacrifice as a religious act. This is important, because the offering of sacrifice formed a vital part of Old Testament worship of God.

(*b*) The Pasch became the most important feast in the Israelite religious year. This was the position it occupied at the coming of Christ—at the transition from Old Testament to New.

(c) Christ himself observed the Pasch. Much more, he took a paschal meal and made it the occasion of the institution of the Eucharist. In other words, Christ deliberately joined together the final Pasch and the first Eucharist.

(d) In this way, the Pasch is one of the strongest links between the Old and New Testaments, and thus we of the New Testament can refer to the heart and kernel of our Christian liturgy as "the Paschal Mystery".

(e) The Bible links the Pasch with the exodus, and thus its organization as an Israelite feast was part of the life-work of Moses. Therefore it is fitting that we should talk about it at this point.

The Concept of Sacrifice

The Pasch was a sacrifice. It is not possible to turn more than a few pages of the Old Testament without being involved in the notion of sacrifice. To get an idea of how prominent a part sacrifice played in the religious life of Israel it is sufficient to read the first seven chapters of the Book of Leviticus. If you wish still further proof, read the final eleven chapters of Leviticus, chapters 17–27. The Book of Leviticus gives a summary view of all Old Testament sacrifices: the different types there were, the victims that could be used, the times of offering, the ritual actions to be carried out, the motives for offering.

But sacrifice is not an exclusively Old Testament feature. Sacrifice is universal. It is a religious element so fundamental to man's nature that sacrifice is found in every religion, even the most exotic, and at every stage of civilization, even the most primitive. Sacrifice is as *old* as religion, and religion is as old as man. Genesis records the sacrifices offered by the patriarchs; the ancient history of Rome, Greece, Babylon tells the same story. Also, sacrifice is as *universal* as religion, and religion is as universal as man. At all times and in all places men have come together and performed some type of action that was directed towards a god. Only an instinct deep in human nature can explain this universality.

In spite of maximum diversity in the actual offering, all sacrifices have a common element and a common purpose. The common element is the giving of something to God; the common purpose is to speak to God, to establish contact with him. A sacrifice, then, is an action that says something to God by means of an external object which is given over to God in some way.

Man has always recognized instinctively his dependence on a higher power. This recognition of man's dependence is, at the same time, a recognition of God's dominion. It is specifically to acknowledge this dependence and dominion that men, everywhere and from the earliest times, have offered sacrifice. A sacrifice, then, must do two things:

1. It must proclaim *God's position* as Lord supreme—and this means adoration and thanksgiving, adoration for what God is, and thanksgiving for what God has done.

2. It must acknowledge *man's position*—and this means begging pardon for the past and help for the future.

Now, these four acts of men—adoration, thanksgiving, expiation and petition—constitute what theologians call the *four ends of sacrifice*, or the motives for offering it. These are the noblest things that a human act can do, but these are the things that sacrifice sets out to do, and that is why men have always looked with reverence on even the simplest act of sacrifice. Even though the god to which it was offered was often false, the sacrifice, the instinct to offer, was true. Beneath the accumulation of myths, rites and cruel practices that have sometimes surrounded sacrifice we find the same God-ward movement of humanity, the desire to say these four things to God. In the Old Testament we find sacrifices designed to transmit one or other of these human messages to God, for example, expiation sacrifices, peace-offerings, thank offerings.

In every sacrifice the message is conveyed by means of an object offered to God as a gift. This gift has taken many forms—a human being, an animal, fruit, corn, wine, property. This is what is called the *victim*. God gave to man all that man has—life and possessions, and man has always felt the desire to give back to God some little gift from his earthly poverty. This something is offered or surrendered to God, and so we always speak of *offering* a sacrifice.

This object is presented by man with the intention that it will be accepted by God. It belongs no more to man but to God. It is now a sacred object, an object that has become God's, and man wants to come as close as possible to this object that has been in contact with divinity. This is the reason for the eating of the victim—the sacrificial element called *communion*, meaning: union with (God).

Since the desire to offer sacrifice is common to all men, it is logical that they should tend to come together as groups and offer a common sacrifice. But an unwieldy group of individuals can perform a common act effectively only when they depute one to act in the name of all. This need to choose one becomes more urgent when men, conscious of their littleness, stand before God, the Supreme. Then they need, not alone an official representative to act for them, but a mediator to stand between them and God; they need a pontifex, a bridge-builder, to span the chasm between the Lord of all and a huddle of confused creatures. This is the offerer of the sacrifice, the *priest*.

Here, then, we have the elements that constitute a sacrifice: a *priest*, acting on behalf of a group, offers to God a *victim*, and this *offering* expresses man's *attitude towards God*. And man's new closeness to God is expressed in the *communion*—the common eating of the consecrated victim. Now, let's look a little closer at this act of offering, the sacred action by which the gift is handed over to God.

Death of the Victim

Since the victim could be living (such as an animal) or inanimate (as are first-fruits), the manner of handing it over to God could be bloody or unbloody. Since God is a Spirit, invisible and intangible, how can man give him something? Man tries to surrender something to God by renouncing it himself. A thing is given to God by being taken, openly and definitively, out of human commerce. The victim is given to God by being withdrawn from normal human currency—by being made useless to man. In unbloody sacrifices, as in the Old Testament sacrifices of first-fruits, of sheaves of corn and of new wine, the victim passes over into God's ownership by being destroyed. Thus, wine and oil were poured out upon the altar. Perhaps the real significance of the Sabbath rest is sacrificial. Here a man offers to God, not an object or an item of property, but a piece of his life. A section of time, a section of a man's life, is renounced and rendered useless to man. One day per week is kept free from contact with work and normal living—it has no commercial value—to show that it is being dedicated to God. It is his day, no longer ours.

However, the highest kind of sacrifice has always involved a living thing—an animal or fowl. And an animate victim passed from man to God only by passing from life to death. The route to God's ownership in this case is the most complete destruction possible, a destruction that is definitive and irrevocable: the death of the victim, the spilling of blood. The death of the victim is the act which expresses the attitude of the offerers.

We can communicate our ideas to one another only by using external signs or acts—words, gestures, gifts. Man tries to communicate with God by the external sign or act of sacrifice—which is the death of the victim. In offering the victim, man is really striving to offer himself to God, perhaps in sorrow for sin, perhaps in thanksgiving. The victim is always a sign of man's inner attitude to God, and here lies the value of sacrifice. It is not the animal, not the shedding of the animal's blood, that gives value to Old Testament sacrifices, but rather the attitude of the men who offered them. This could be an attitude of contrition—and then the blood of the victim flows that the blood of sinners may be spared. The attitude could be one of petition—and the sacrifice is death-dealing to the victim that it may be life-giving to the offerer. The attitude could also be one of thanksgiving—and man offers the victim as an offering of himself in gratitude. Or, finally, an attitude of adoration—and then the victim passes over into the hands of God as a symbol of man's need and man's desire to make the same journey. And when men sit down together to eat the flesh of the victim, the wheel has come full circle. What they have given to God, he now gives back to them—joining them to himself like members of the same family clustered around the common table. An insignificant human offering had set out from men towards God; now a divine gift has come down from God to men.

Sacrifice, then, under its great diversity of forms, is always man's attempt to construct a Jacob's ladder between earth and heaven.

Origin of the Pasch

With these general ideas of sacrifice, its meaning and its motive, we can now proceed to examine one particular Old Testament sacrifice, the Pasch. The Bible introduces us to the Pasch in Exodus 12. We have already spoken of this chapter in connection with the tenth plague, the death of the Egyptian firstborn, and with the liberation of the Israelites from Egypt. The Pasch, then, comes on the scene at this dramatic moment when the descendants of Abraham, Isaac and Jacob are at a crossroads in their history, when nine plagues have failed to soften Pharaoh's heart and their trust in Moses is at its lowest. We cannot improve on the Bible's simple, unsophisticated account, so at this point you should read Exodus 12 (vv. 1–14 and 21–27).

From the details given in these verses we can reconstruct the Israelite paschal supper. It was to be celebrated on the evening of the fourteenth day of the first month of the year. This was the month of Abib (=month of corn), later called the month Nisan, and it corresponds to our March-April. Since they followed a lunar calendar, the first day of the month Abib coincided with a new moon, and thus the fourteenth was always the night of the full moon. Each family chose a lamb "without blemish, a male a year old"; in other words, they chose a valuable animal from the flock, and thus a meaningful renunciation for the family, and a gift worthy to offer to God. The lamb was killed at twilight and its blood sprinkled over the lintel of the door, but obviously sprinkled originally on the tentpoles during the desert wanderings. The meat was roasted, no bone of the animal being broken (*Exod.* 12:46); it was to be eaten immediately, and anything that remained over had to be burnt—so that it could not be used for a profane meal. With it they eat unleavened bread, which is bread to which no yeast had been added, and "bitter herbs", the desert plants that the Bedouin use to season food. All taking part in the meal were to be in travelling dress, which meant with their long flowing robes tucked up under their belts, not barefooted but wearing sandals, and with their shepherds' long walking-sticks in their hands—in other words, as if ready to set out at once on a journey.

From the structure of the ceremony, it is obviously a sacrifice offered by nomads, by shepherds. Many details of the rite converge on this conclusion. There is no need for altar or priest, indicating that it originated in a very primitive stage of society. The lamb is cooked on an open fire, and in the open air. Nomads had few, if any, kitchen utensils, and none are needed here— which is why no bone of the animal need be broken. The meat is eaten with unleavened bread—then as now, the bread of the desert Bedouin; it is eaten with bitter herbs, the tough diminutive plants that grow even in the Sinai and Arabian deserts; it is eaten at full moon—the brightest night of the month for those whose home is a tent. From all this we can conclude that the Pasch is a very ancient feast, going back to the time when the Israelites were still semi-nomadic. Most probably, this was a feast originally celebrated as the shepherd tribes struck camp before leaving with their flocks for the new spring pastures, and it was probably celebrated by Semites all over the Near East.

Pasch and Exodus

What we have just said would mean that the Pasch existed before the exodus and outside of Israel. What, then, is the meaning of Exodus 12, where the Pasch is imposed on the Israelites as a perpetual memorial service of the exodus? The correct relationship between the Pasch and the exodus seems to be this. The Pasch was a common oriental springtime feast. One springtime in the thirteenth century B.C. there took place one of God's great acts in history, by which he accomplished the liberation of the Israelites from Egypt. This liberation was both political and religious; it meant freedom from a tyrannical Pharaoh, and freedom to worship Yahweh, their God. It marked the beginning of Israel as the Chosen People, and, as an historical event, dominated the whole history of salvation. It is only natural that Israel should recall it and celebrate it in some solemn manner, and the most solemn manner they knew of was by sacrifice. It remained, then, to find a suitable sacrifice, and this they found by borrowing the existing paschal feast. Its structure, as a feast of desert nomads, made it an admirably suitable commemoration of an event that compelled the Israelites to be nomads in the Sinai desert for a generation. From this time onwards, the springtime ceremony of the Pasch took on, for the Israelites, an entirely new significance— it became their official religious memorial of the exodus. Its original function was entirely overshadowed, and so, in the final editing of the Pentateuch, the Pasch was put into the historical setting of the exodus. That was the significance it held in the consciousness of Israel—it was the feast of the liberation.

What we have in Exodus 12, then, is neither the complete creation of a new ceremony, nor the passive borrowing of an existing one. It is the adaptation by Israel of an ancient and venerable rite to a new purpose and to the true God. The old rite is given a new and nobler meaning—and we shall see this happen again later on, when the paschal lamb becomes Christ and the paschal supper becomes the Eucharist.

Pasch in Israel's History

From Exodus 12 we can distinguish the following as the five essential characteristics of the Pasch:

1. A sacrifice, having a lamb as victim;
2. Specific use of blood as an agent of preservation from the anger of Yahweh;

3. A domestic or family banquet, not a public temple one;
4. Signifying liberation from a state of servitude;
5. Signifying the beginning of a new era—that of the People of God.

These five elements continue right through the Bible story, and the alterations that the paschal rite underwent through the centuries do not affect this central structure. Between the exodus and the birth of Christ, Israel celebrated over 1,200 paschal suppers. The Old Testament mentions only a few specific Paschs, but they are significant ones, because each one not alone commemorates the exodus from Egypt, but each is itself the occasion of a new liberation and a new beginning. It may be helpful to glance at a few examples.

Joshua 5 tells of the first Pasch in the Promised Land. "While the people of Israel were encamped in Gilgal they kept the Passover on the fourteenth day of the month at evening in the plains of Jericho" (v. 10). This Pasch was celebrated, then, only a few miles from the Jordan, which the Israelites have just crossed for the first time. They have been rescued from their enemies in Transjordan, liberated from the hazards of the desert, and they are beginning a new era in the salvation story—the People of Yahweh in their Promised Land.

2 Kings 23 describes the celebration of the Pasch in the religious reformation of King Josiah. We shall speak about Josiah again, because he was one of the good and kindly kings of Judah. Vv. 21–22 tell us: "And the king commanded all the people, 'Keep the passover to the Lord your God, as it is written in this book of the covenant.' For no such passover had been kept since the days of the judges . . ." This does not necessarily mean that the Pasch had lapsed; more probably it means that the Pasch under Josiah was in some way a new one, with some new element. This new Pasch was celebrated about 620 B.C. What is new about it is that now the Pasch will be celebrated, not wherever a man lives, but in the city of Jerusalem. It is now a pilgrimage feast—all Jews must come together to Jerusalem and there hold the supper. This is how the Pasch continued to be celebrated; this is what we

find at the time of Christ. In this Pasch of good King Josiah we find again the note of a deliverance and a new beginning—deliverance from the idolatry into which Judah had fallen, and a new beginning in the service of Yahweh.

Finally, Ezra 6 tells of the first Pasch after the return from the Babylonian captivity. The Jews who had been scattered are being gathered together; the faith that had been shattered is being re-organized, and as part of that process we find the celebration of the Pasch in Jerusalem about 500 B.C. Again the significance is: the new liberation from exile in Babylon, and the new beginning of the remnant of Israel in Jerusalem.

But whether the Pasch was being celebrated on some great historic occasion, or on an ordinary unspectacular year, its chief function was to commemorate the exodus. It drew its importance, not from its own nature or its own ritual, but from the exodus. And because it was the memorial of the exodus it came to be the most important single feast in the life of the good Israelite, and this is the position it occupied in the religion of Israel as we cross the threshold into the New Testament.

Pasch at the Time of Christ

Naturally, with the passage of the centuries the structure of the feast was altered slightly to allow some additions, and to adapt it to a temple-dominated religion. At the time of Christ, the lamb was generally bought in the temple courtyard; John 2 tells how Christ drove out the sellers of the lambs on the first Pasch of his public ministry. The lamb was killed by a priest, and its blood sprinkled on the altar of holocausts. Then it was brought back to the family or group to which it belonged. These were some of the preparations that Christ sent Peter and John to carry out before the Last Supper (*Luke* 22). By this time, too, the paschal supper had become a fuller and a longer meal. It began, like all Jewish meals, with a washing of hands. It involved the drinking of four cups of wine, to which a little water had been added, spaced at intervals during the traditional meal. Then to the material elements of the meal was added the solemn declaration in words of what it all meant. The youngest boy in the family gathering asked the head of the household: What is the meaning of this service? And the host replied by telling the story of the exodus and the first Pasch. The whole ceremony came to a close with the singing of a group of Psalms (Pss. 113–18), one of which (Ps. 114) is the song of the exodus story. Thus the ceremony of the paschal supper had what we might call "matter and form"—actions and words—all speaking to every true Israelite of Egypt, the Sea of Reeds, the desert, and the strength and goodness of God's right hand.

The Last Supper

St John mentions three Paschs in Christ's public ministry, but only one of these receives detailed attention from all four Evangelists. This is the final Pasch, the occasion of the Last Supper and the death of Christ. What we call the Last Supper was in fact the celebration of the Pasch, complete with lamb, unleavened bread, etc. Like all good Jews, Christ and the Apostles had come to Jerusalem to celebrate it. The Pasch is a family celebration, and Christ and the Apostles shape themselves into a little family gathering in the upper room of an unnamed friend, Christ acting as head of the household, the Apostles as members of a family.

To this paschal supper "on the night when he was betrayed" Christ joined two things: (i) the institution of the Eucharist; (ii) the commencement of his passion. And by doing this he gave to the ancient Pasch an entirely new meaning and function. Just as Moses, at the time of the exodus, had taken an existing ceremony and transformed it into something higher, so now Christ takes the Old Testament Pasch and transforms it beyond all human dreams. He does more than that; at the Last Supper he gives to the Old Testament Pasch its historical and religious fulfilment. The Pasch was one of the things that he came not to abolish but to fulfil. He who had already claimed to be Lord of the Sabbath now showed himself Lord also of the Pasch. This he did in two ways: by instituting the permanent Eucharist in the context of the paschal meal, and by identifying himself as the reality foreshadowed for centuries by the paschal lamb.

When we read the four gospel accounts of the Last Supper we see how Christ observed the ritual of the paschal meal, and adapted its elements to found a new rite and announce a new liberation. To the washing of hands which opened the meal Christ added the washing of his Apostles' feet. The dish of bitter herbs gave him the opportunity of announcing his approaching death and the betrayal of Judas. As head of the little group it was his duty to tell the story of the exodus, and to this he added the explanation of his death—the long sermon in John 14–17. Over a morsel of the unleavened bread he pronounced the momentous words: This is my body; over one of the cups of wine the words: This is my blood of the new covenant. And the little ceremony concluded with the singing of the Hallel Psalms: "And when they had sung a hymn, they went out to the Mount of Olives" (*Mark* 14:26).

At the Last Supper, Christ transformed the old Pasch into a new one. The shadows gave way to the realities—and so perfectly. Christ presented himself as the new and eternal Paschal Lamb, the supreme victim. Three years earlier John the Baptist had pointed to him with the words: "Behold, the Lamb of God", but only now do we see the real significance of this mysterious phrase. On Good Friday, his blood will be shed as the blood of the paschal lamb was shed—and for the same purpose: to ward off the punishment of God. When the legs of the two thieves are broken and Christ's are not, St John points out the parallel with the ancient lamb. "For these things took place that the scripture might be fulfilled, 'Not a bone of him shall be broken'" (*John* 19:36). About thirty years later, St Paul will crystallize all this into one of those short, sharp sayings of his: "Christ, our paschal lamb, has been sacrificed" (1 *Cor.* 5:7).

The Old Testament Pasch was more than sacrifice; it was a meal, a sacrificial meal in which several people shared in eating the flesh of the victim. By the institution of the Eucharist, the last meal in Christ's public life became the first banquet in the life of his Church. He took the unleavened bread of the old Pasch, but when he broke it and gave it to his Apostles it was no longer the

grim fare of the desert. It was now his own Body, the flesh of the
new Paschal Lamb. The Eucharist, like the Pasch, is sacrament as
well as sacrifice; it will be the nourishment of the new Israel. The
transformation of the paschal meal was now complete. There was
but one thing left to do, and that was to command that this rite,
now so rich in meaning, be repeated. Moses had ordered that the
Pasch be perpetually repeated in memory of the exodus: "You
shall observe this rite as an ordinance for you and for your sons
for ever" (*Exod.* 12:24). At the Last Supper Christ orders that the
new Pasch, the Eucharist, be repeated in memory of his death:
"Do this in remembrance of me."

Thus we find in the Last Supper and the passion the same five
essential elements that the Pasch contained: sacrifice, the use of
blood, a family banquet, a liberation and a new beginning.

Pasch in the Christian Life

And the Pasch continues. Holy Week and the resurrection are
not Christ's glorification alone; they are the liberation of the
people of the new Israel, the Church. St Paul insists, in season
and out of season, that the Eucharist is the new Pasch, grace is the
new exodus, and baptism is our crossing of the Sea of Reeds.
Baptism is the death and resurrection of Christ applied to the

Pasch	In life of Israel	In life of Christ	In life of Christians
Banquet ..	Supper	Last Supper ..	Eucharist—as sacrament
Sacrifice ..	Lamb ..	Death of Christ	Eucharist—as sacrifice of Mass
Liberation ..	Exodus ..	Resurrection ..	Baptism
New Beginning	People of God	Christian Era	Life of Grace

individual soul, bringing to that soul liberation from sin and the new beginning of the life of grace and friendship with God. This is what the difficult chapter six of the Epistle to the Romans is saying.

From this vantage-point we get yet another glimpse of how the salvation story unfolds, and of the continuity between the successive stages of the divine plan.

By celebrating together in the upper room the final Pasch and the first Eucharist, Christ forged a visible ritual link between the two Testaments, joining together the old sacrifice of Israel and the new sacrifice of the Christian era of grace. He chose, in dying, to link his death with the Old Testament Pasch. In this way, he gathered up a whole section of Israelite religion and christianized it. Thus the tide of sacred history, from Moses to Christ, from Sinai to upper room, rolls on unbroken—right to us.

CHAPTER 6

In the Land of Canaan

Reading: Numbers, chapters, 10–32
Deuteronomy, chapter 34
Joshua, chapters 3–11
Judges, chapters 4–16
Ecclesiasticus, chapter 46
Psalm 136

THE Sinai Covenant has linked God and man together in a new manner and a new relationship. The Hebrews are now Yahweh's chosen people, and the rest of the salvation plan will be worked out through them. This does not mean that all other men on the face of the earth were excluded from God's care and friendship, but rather that his blessings would ultimately reach them by means of his elected race. How this would be achieved, however, did not become evident until the New Testament and Christ's foundation of a universal Church.

In the meantime, Yahweh's people are a landless and defence-less tribe encamped in the inhospitable wilderness of the Sinai Peninsula. They cannot grow and prosper if they are to continue as manna-fed and tent-dwelling wanderers. They need a land of their own, a slice of territory where they can settle permanently and serve their God in security and peace. Six centuries earlier, Yahweh had told Abraham: "Arise, walk through the length and the breadth of the land, for I will give it to you" (*Gen.* 13:17).

And so they set their faces towards that long-promised land, Canaan—which we now call Palestine.

What we shall be talking about in this chapter, then, is the transition of the Hebrews from a tribe into a nation. By taking possession of the land of Canaan the people of Yahweh became also the nation of Yahweh. Because this transition was a milestone in their development, the later Israelite historians wrote of it at length. That is why we must read a rather large amount of the biblical text in order to cover this period. Leaving aside the elements of legislation that are intermixed with the historical narrative, we see that there are three distinct stages in the biblical sequence:

1. *Moses* completes his task and takes the Hebrews to the east bank of the Jordan. This is described in detail in Numbers 10–32; and a later writer's summary of it is found in Deuteronomy 1–4. Deuteronomy 34 records the death of Moses.
2. The military career and achievements of *Joshua* form the subject of Joshua 3–11.
3. The most important of the *Judges* are spoken of in the central section of the Book of Judges, chapters 4–16.

The Desert Odyssey

After the long and eventful period at Sinai, the Hebrews are finally ready to leave, and Numbers 10 takes up the story of their journey. Most of the details of it are familiar to us since the pre-Sinai march. They are led by the same pillar of cloud and of fire, they are fed by the same manna, they make the same mistakes and they show the same lack of faith in Yahweh and in Moses. In short, they continued to enjoy constant and unwavering divine protection, and to demonstrate incorrigible human fickleness. It took all the strength and tenacity of Moses to hold them together and to centre their faith on Yahweh.

One of the most effective instruments in this process was the Tabernacle. This they had constructed during their stay near the base of Mount Sinai. It was simply a big tent, and its appearance and size are described in Exodus from chapter 25 to the end. It was the best tent that they could make in the circumstances; it was probably, at least to our eyes, an incongruous assortment of goatskins and precious metals, presumably the ones they had brought with them from Egypt (*Exod.* 12:35–6). But whatever it looked like, they had lavished on it all the care and skill of which they were capable. It housed the Ark of the Covenant, their most treasured possession, it was their place of religious assembly, and it represented the presence of God among them. It was their first temple; in fact, Solomon's later temple in Jerusalem was merely an elaborate facsimile in stone and timber of the crude Tabernacle of the desert. It is good to remember, as we read the Exodus text, that the Tabernacle was the first "house of God" on earth, the first church where the people of God assembled, and that it meant to the Hebrews all that the soaring cathedrals of the middle ages meant to Christian Europe. It was more than a place of prayer—it was the centre of gravity of their whole religious attitude.

Numbers 10 suggests that they had spent more than a year close to Mount Sinai, and so they are only in the second year of their desert odyssey when they leave Sinai and "march from the mount of the Lord three days' journey" (v. 33). This section of the Old Testament leaves us with two general impressions of the next period in their career: (a) that it lasted forty years; (b) that it was spent in continuous movement from place to place.

(a) Obviously, nobody will take the number forty as an exact tally. It is a conveniently round number, and besides it is a favourite biblical number. A forty-year period is approximately the space of time that we would describe as a "generation", i.e. the period that elapses between the time at which a man becomes head of a family group and the time at which his son succeeds him as head. Thus, we can take it to mean that a generation of Hebrews spent their lives on the journey from Egypt to Canaan, and in fact this is stated explicitly in Numbers 14:31-2: "But your little ones, who you said would become a prey, I will bring in, and they shall know the land which you have despised. But as for you, your dead bodies shall fall in this wilderness."

The Hebrews who crossed the Jordan with Joshua were a new generation, the sons of those who had followed Moses across the Sea of Reeds.

In later Israelite thought, the number forty came to be associated with a period spent in desert surroundings. Thus we find Elijah the prophet journeying into the wilderness for forty days (1 *Kings*

19:8), and Christ "in the wilderness forty days" (*Mark* 1:13). In our Christian liturgy, the Lenten season of forty days echoes the same thought. Alert readers will find many other instances, as in Deuteronomy 9:18—Moses forty days on the mountain.

(*b*) Many passages in the Pentateuch give the impression that their whole period in the desert was spent in a kind of aimless wandering from place to place—a series of purposeless circles. Numbers 33, for example, gives a list of the different places where they camped: "These are the stages of the people of Israel, when they went forth out of the land of Egypt." It is an impressive list of names (and we are not surprised to find that the "stages" are forty in number!), but it is quite pointless to attempt to trace the sequence of encampments. For one thing, many of these places cannot be identified with certainty now. Next, even among those which can be located the sequence given in the text provides a most improbable series of criss-cross marches.

We need hardly feel obliged to accept such lists of place-names as an accurate and orderly account of their stopping-places. We shall see in a later chapter that this account was written down long after the events had taken place. It was written down by men who had no personal experience or knowledge of the topography of the Sinai Peninsula. The names had come to them by oral tradition, handed down from one generation to the next in long narrative forms that enshrined all they knew of the history of their race. The writers faithfully record the place-names as they receive them, but they do not attempt the impossible—to put them into correct historical and geographical order. A faint analogy might be the case of many Americans of Irish descent who speak with eloquence and affection of the beauties of Killarney, Connemara and the hills of Donegal, without having clear ideas of where exactly in Ireland these places are.

At Kadesh

Several hints in the text have led modern scholars to conclude that in fact the Hebrews spent most of this desert period encamped at a place called Kadesh, between Mount Sinai and the southern frontier of Canaan. It is still a welcome oasis of green trees and running water—and is still called 'Ain Qadeis. They seem to have made Kadesh a permanent base from which they moved out occasionally, as the needs of pasturing their flocks dictated, but to which they returned again. This period spent at Kadesh was an important stage in their transition into nationhood, because it was yet another providential preparation for their future destiny. It gave them the opportunity to become accustomed to their new freedom, to act as free men making responsible decisions rather than as slaves dependent on the whims of a tyrant. It presented them with the need and the occasion to meditate on, and put into execution, the new covenant of Sinai; as a result, much of the legislation in the Pentateuch took its first rough shape probably during this period.

But every human story is one of light and shadow. The Sinai alliance with Yahweh had indeed changed their destiny—but not their human nature. And so we find this period of their history marked by almost continuous grumbling, and several open and defiant rebellions against Moses. Their complaints are interesting, even amusing, and certainly unoriginal. Numbers 11 does not mince words. "Now the rabble that was among them had a strong craving; and the people of Israel also wept again, and said, 'O that we had meat to eat! We remember the fish we ate in Egypt for nothing, the cucumbers, the melons, the leeks, the onions, and the garlic; but now our strength is dried up, and there is nothing at all but this manna to look at' " (vv. 4–6).

Even those closest to Moses, his brother and official assistant, Aaron, and his sister Miriam, "spoke against Moses", and Numbers 12 describes how "the anger of the Lord was kindled against them". But when Miriam develops leprosy, it is Moses who prays for her: "And Moses cried to the Lord, 'Heal her, O God, I beseech you' " (v. 13). Rarely does an Old Testament writer allow himself the luxury of a personal comment, but perhaps this is one exception. In Numbers 12:3 we find a note of admiration, almost of wonderment: "Now the man Moses was very meek, more than all men that were on the face of the earth."

While based at Kadesh, Moses sends a group to take a first

look at this promised land so direly needed and so ardently desired. Numbers 13 tells how Moses chose one man from each of the tribal groups—a shrewd piece of practical wisdom, because spying, then as now, was a hazardous occupation, and he did not wish to have the best men in a single group wiped out. Furtively the spies crossed over the southern frontier of Canaan and spent some time (conveniently called forty days, v. 25) wandering about the valleys and low hills, in the guise of innocent nomads. Then they returned "to Moses and Aaron and to all the congregation of the people of Israel in the wilderness of Paran, at Kadesh" (v. 26), and made their report. "We came to the land to which you sent us; it flows with milk and honey, and this is its fruit. Yet the people who dwell in the land are strong, and the cities are fortified and very large; and besides, we saw the descendants of Anak there" (vv. 27-8).

Despite the strain of poetic exaggeration, this description of Canaan was, in their circumstances, quite realistic. By contrast with the arid and unfriendly desert, the gentle green slopes of Palestine suggested abundance and fertility. And by contrast with the unarmed mob that clustered around Moses, the citizens of the walled towns must have seemed as impregnable as mythical giants.

This report provoked mixed reactions among the "congregation" at Kadesh. "But Caleb quieted the people before Moses, and said, 'Let us go up at once, and occupy it; for we are well able to overcome it.' Then the men who had gone up with him said, 'We are not able to go up against the people; for they are stronger than we'" (vv. 30-1).

There will always be two classes of men. In this case, the sad thing was that both groups seemed to have forgotten that Yahweh was their God, their guide and their protector. The brave trusted in themselves, and the faint-hearted could only whine: "Would that we had died in the land of Egypt!" It is not surprising that Numbers 14 says: "And the Lord said to Moses, 'How long will this people despise me? And how long will they not believe in me, in spite of all the signs which I have wrought among them?'" (v. 11). And once again the rebellious Hebrews paid the price for ignoring Yahweh, their God. The despairing "died by plague before the Lord" (v. 37); the presumptuous still insisted on attacking Canaan and had to beat an inglorious retreat: "Then the Amalekites and the Canaanites who dwelt in that hill country came down, and defeated them and pursued them, even to Hormah" (v. 45).

Such was the general pattern of the desert period: a recurring cycle of divine blessing, human gratitude, then human frailty and rebellion, divine punishment, human repentance, divine pardon and blessing—and then the cycle begins all over again. The history of Israel as recorded in the books we are going to read next—Joshua, Judges, Samuel and Kings—takes the form of a repeated series of such cycles of divine goodness and human fickleness. It is approximately the form that all human history takes; it is this that makes all history a continuous monument to the patience and love of Yahweh for all the creatures of his choice.

On the March

By the time the Hebrews finally begin the journey towards Canaan, they have drawn some practical conclusions from their experiences in and around Kadesh. First, they now know that only a military campaign of some kind will win them their Promised Land. That they made some primitive attempt to shape themselves into an army is proved by the fact that, in Numbers 21, they clash with the Amorites and emerge victorious—"And Israel slew him with the edge of the sword" (v. 24). This was their first military victory, and must have been a source of hope and courage for the difficult days ahead.

Secondly, they had discovered that there was little hope in attacking the southern border of Canaan; they had no stomach for a second defeat by the Amalekites. So they now take a long detour around by the southern shore of the Dead Sea, and then push their way slowly up through Transjordan, until eventually they are encamped in the high plains of Moab, whence they can gaze across the river at their cherished home. It is in this region, and at this point, that we bid farewell to Moses.

His death at the very threshold of Palestine has often left readers with a certain feeling of bafflement. Again and again the

text says that Moses was not allowed to enter Canaan. The phrase
of Deuteronomy 3:27 is typical: "Go up to the top of Pisgah, and
lift up your eyes westward and northward and southward and
eastward, and behold it with your eyes; for you shall not go over
this Jordan."

At the same time, the text contains evidence that the biblical
writers did not have clear ideas about the reason for this strange
decision. You can easily verify this for yourself. Generally they
speak of it as a punishment because of an incident in Numbers 20,
where Moses is commanded to strike a rock in order to provide
water for the Hebrews and their flocks. The description of the
incident is given in verses 6-11. And in these verses there is no
indication that Moses sinned or erred in any way. Still, verse 12
accuses him of lack of faith in Yahweh, and verse 24 calls it lack of
obedience to Yahweh. Later on, Deuteronomy 1:37 says that
Moses is being punished because of the people's sinfulness.
Psalm 106:33 gives yet another reason: "he spoke words that
were rash." This is sufficient to show that, while the Israelites
marvelled at Moses' exclusion from Canaan, they did not know
the precise cause of it. We are in the same position.

For many pages now we have been following the career of
Moses—from his birth on the banks of the Nile to his death on the
mount of Nebo; in fact, the distance between these two points
constitutes his life and achievement. All that we might wish to say
of him has been well expressed in the words which bring the
Pentateuch to a close. "And there has not arisen a prophet since
in Israel like Moses, whom the Lord knew face to face, none like
him for all the signs and the wonders which the Lord sent him to
do in the land of Egypt, to Pharaoh and to all his servants and to
all his land, and for all the mighty power and all the great and
terrible deeds which Moses wrought in the sight of all Israel"
(*Deut*. 34:10–12). This was Israel's memory of Moses—and it is
ours.

The Campaign of Joshua

When Joshua succeeds to the leadership of the Hebrews he is
not by any means a newcomer to the scene. He has already been

mentioned several times in the Book of Exodus, and always in a context which shows that he was Moses' trusted lieutenant; as in Exodus 17 which introduces him as Commander-in-Chief of the little Hebrew army, and in Exodus 24, already familiar to us, we find Joshua side-by-side with Moses on this momentous occasion (v. 13). The name "Joshua" is an abbreviation of two Hebrew words meaning "Yahweh is salvation"; "Jesus" is simply the Greek form of this same name.

On this man falls the honour and the burden of facing an unknown country and conquering it for his followers against, in human terms, insuperable odds. But his name was also his encouragement—Yahweh, not Joshua, would guide his people to final safety. This was the first message that Joshua transmitted to his people: "The Lord your God is providing you a place of rest, and will give you this land" (*Jos.* 1:13).

The Book of Joshua is easy to read, and we need say little about it. Always when we come to read a book of the Bible, it is best to begin by dividing it into sections. As we turn the pages of Joshua, we see immediately how easily it falls into clearly-defined sections or "chapters" (the biblical chapters, a medieval addition to the text, are not always the best possible division).

Section I—First Foothold:
    Chapters 1–2: Joshua's appointment and first preparations for an assault on Canaan.
    Chapters 3–4: The crossing of the river Jordan.
    Chapter 5: Religious rites of consecration to Yahweh.

Section II—Campaign of Conquest:
    Chapters 6–9: Central Canaan, e.g. Jericho.
    Chapter 10: Southern Canaan, e.g. Lachish.
    Chapter 11: Northern Canaan, e.g. Hazor.

Section III—Settlement of the Tribes:
    Chapters 13–22.

Now, it is not necessary to conclude that the events of this troubled period were as neatly organized in their happening as in their telling. It is possible that the settlement of a group followed immediately on the conquest of a piece of territory sufficient to support it. In fact, this must have been a military necessity, to prevent the conquered territory from falling again into Canaanite hands.

Similarly, it is hardly necessary to accept that Joshua's campaign was skilfully and deliberately divided into the three sections covering central, southern and northern Canaan. As we remarked already in connection with the desert "wanderings", it is important to remember that the Book of Joshua was written several centuries after the events it records. In the meantime, the historical facts had been handed down from generation to generation by word of mouth, stored up and kept fresh in the memory of Israel. When they did finally come to write them down, they did not set out to present an ordered chronological and geographical sequence of details, as, for example, a modern historian would do if writing about World War I. Instead, they set down the historical facts in what we would call epic form, which means a narrative style that tends to simplify the events and glorify the persons. Rather than chronicle, step by painful step, the slow progress of Joshua, the book seems afire with enthusiasm as it rushes breathlessly from one Israelite victory to another. That the victories finally were theirs is certain, but we are free to doubt that they came as rapidly and resoundingly as an unwary reading of the Book of Joshua would suggest. And the careful reader will notice that Joshua 13:1-6 emphasizes that much of the land of Canaan was still unconquered at the end of the campaign.

The Land of Promise

To understand and enjoy the Joshua story we need to take a long hard look at a map of Palestine. Fortunately, Palestine is an easy country to get to know, whether one's tour is by armchair or autobus. First, it is a small country; its maximum length is about 150 miles, and its width ranges from 25 to 90 miles. Including the territory east of the Jordan, its total area is about 9,700 square miles—less than one-third the size of Ireland. That so tiny a country could have exerted such tremendous influence on history

has always seemed little short of miraculous; in the fifth century
A.D. St Jerome said that he hesitated to talk about the size of
Palestine "lest we should seem to be furnishing pagans with an
opportunity for mockery". Next, it is a country of simple
geographical structure. It consists of three parallel layers, running
from north to south. In the west, by the Mediterranean, there is a
coastal plain, a narrow strip of pleasant and fertile country. East
of this there is a central mountain range, rugged and difficult to
cultivate. And finally there is the low valley of the Jordan, a green
and friendly area in its northern section, but a parched and
sweltering desert farther south around the shores of the Dead Sea.

This, then, is the Land of Promise, and it is not difficult to
imagine the surge of joy and gratitude in the hearts of the weary
Israelites as they finally waded across the river Jordan. As we
noticed already in connection with the crossing of the Sea of
Reeds, the Bible does not pause to discuss the exact nature of the
event by which they were enabled to cross over. By some combination of physical circumstances, all carefully plotted by a
loving Yahweh, they found themselves standing "in the plains of
Jericho". At long last, Yahweh's children were home again—back
on the soil which Jacob and his sons had left over four hundred
years earlier. It was a historic moment for them; they had
emerged from the mouth of a long and darksome tunnel into
which they had plunged at the Sea of Reeds. And, as they did on
all such historic occasions, they celebrated it by religious rites—
described in Joshua 5. They celebrated the Pasch, solemn reminder of the initial liberation that had made this day possible.
They renewed the ceremony of circumcision, the external sign
that they were the people covenanted to Yahweh, the proof that
they were truly the sons of Abraham and the servants of the God
of Abraham. It may be useful to re-read here Genesis 17:1–14,
the passage that describes how circumcision is "a sign of the
covenant". They also set up twelve stones from the river-bed to
form a perpetual monument to their new homeland.

Since the beginning of the century, archeologists have combined science with hard and patient work in excavating biblical
sites in Palestine, and have assembled a body of information that

throws much light on the invasion of Joshua. The results of many archeological campaigns have both confirmed and amplified the biblical account, and have established its date as the thirteenth century B.C. Like most readers of the Bible, archeologists were particularly intrigued by Joshua 6—the dramatic fate of Jericho. This city, only six miles from the Jordan, was the first test of Israelite skill and courage against the walled cities of Canaan. But while Jericho was a heart-warming victory for the Israelites, it has been a disappointment to archeologists. Since 1907, successive teams have worked among these ancient ruins, and, to date, they have found no trace of the city or the walls that fell to Joshua in the thirteenth century. There is, in the excavated ruins, an extraordinary gap, extending over several hundreds of years, and including the very period in which we are interested—the age of Joshua. Thus, neither the biblical text nor modern science gives us sufficient information to say exactly how and why the walls of Jericho fell down. We must, for the present at least, be content with the knowledge that the city fell to the Israelite besiegers—which perhaps is all that the text of Joshua 6 wishes to tell us.

The third section of the Book of Joshua does not make very exciting reading, as chapters 13–22 are a dull litany of place-names, setting out in detail how the captured territory of Canaan was shared out among the twelve tribes of Israel. A few remarks suffice on this section.

It is probably at this time that the people began to refer to themselves exclusively as "Israelites". Up to this they were called Hebrews, at least generally; this was a term that designated nomads or desert people. In other words, it described them rather than identified them. But "Israelites" became their proper name; and it was more than merely a national name—it meant those who were aggregated to the people of Yahweh. As far as we can gather, it was thus chiefly a religious term. And it is the name by which they shall be known until the closing centuries of the Old Testament. It is probably at this time also that a definite division into twelve tribes became an established fact. Even though reference to the twelve-fold division, based on the families of the sons of Jacob, is found earlier in the Bible story, it seems more likely that they emerged as distinct and independent groups only in the division of the land.

We are sometimes tempted to ask why a historical writer, especially one interested specifically in salvation history, should squander so much space on detailed lists of place-names. Perhaps the correct answer is the simplest and most obvious one—that in the meditation of Israel on God's saving ways, every inch of the Promised Land was another proof of his love, and therefore treasured and loved. They repeat, with obvious affection, the names of towns, cities and valleys—in a kind of roll-call of national honour. Names like Anathoth, Dan, Beth-horon, Hebron, Ramath —these they repeated lovingly as if tasting once again the sweet savour of victory.

The Judges of Israel

What, then, was the Israelite situation at the death of Joshua? It was obviously an immense improvement on the state of affairs he had inherited from Moses at the foot of Mount Nebo. But his conquest of Canaan was only a partial conquest, and many battles had to be fought and several centuries pass before the Israelites were masters of the land. The twelve tribes were scattered at both sides of the Jordan, each holding on grimly to a piece of territory. In between, several unconquered pockets of Canaanites remained. This situation was fraught with dangers of several kinds for the Israelites. Each of the twelve scattered tribes must fend for itself as best it can. Their isolation from one another made their military position extremely precarious. Living in a sea of pagan neighbours made their religious situation equally dangerous, as the temptation to worship the false Canaanite gods was a constant and a pressing one. And, with the death of Joshua, they found themselves for the first time without a leader.

Without a unifying force, and without any central leadership, the twelve tribes gradually began to lose their unity and their identity as a people, and the crusading spirit with which they had forded the Jordan slowly ebbed away. It is against this background that we must read the story told in the Book of Judges. That story covers the period from about 1200 to 1020 B.C.—almost 200 years. The text itself makes it abundantly clear that this was an era of insecurity and almost of chaos for tiny Israel. The ex-nomads, struggling to keep their toe-hold in Palestine and to adapt themselves to their new way of life, oscillated constantly between mastery and abject defeat. They sorely missed the discipline imposed on their fathers by Moses and later by Joshua. Judges 17:6 is almost ominous in its curt description of that chaotic time. "In those days there was no king in Israel; every man did what was right in his own eyes." And, lest we miss the point, the book concludes with the very same phrase (*Judg.* 21:25).

But Yahweh could not and did not abandon his people. This time he came to their rescue by raising up a number of courageous figures that the Old Testament calls "judges". The term "judge" has little or no judicial connotation in their case; that they judged in our sense of the word is mentioned only of two of them, Deborah and Samuel. In reality, they were primarily military leaders, liberators, local heroes who rallied a tribe or group of tribes in face of an enemy threat. In this time of confusion they anticipated the functions of both king and prophet, because they led their followers to victory and thereby championed the cause of Yahweh. They were the providential remedy for the helplessness of the Israelites, and in no other nation of the ancient orient do we find a corresponding group. In the grand design of the Old Testament their function was to consolidate and complete the work begun by Joshua, and to ensure that the Israelites would possess the land of Canaan, not as tenants but as masters.

The Book of Judges describes the achievements of twelve judges, but it is obvious that six of them are important figures, while the other six receive rather scant treatment. Of the six major judges, everybody should enjoy reading the history of Deborah (chapters 4–5), Gideon (chapters 6–8) and Samson (chapters 13–16). Deborah, the only female judge, is introduced (in 4:4) by a rather unusual phrase: "She used to sit under the palm of Deborah between Ramah and Bethel in the hill country of Ephraim." This is not an indication of a life of indolent leisure, but rather that she was a recognized arbitrator in disputes of social

7

and family life, a "judge" in our sense, holding court in the shade of a certain tree. But when the need arose, she abandoned the palm tree rather quickly and led an Israelite army to victory in the battle of the river Kishon. This battle and its result are described in chapter 4 in the historian's prose, but in chapter 5 in a much older version—one of the most martial, most lively and most lovely pieces of poetry in the Old Testament. Please read the fifth chapter—and out loud if possible, the better to savour the rugged, primitive beauty of it.

However, the Judges never exerted more than a local influence. No one of them succeeded in exercising authority over a united Israel, and so some other and more permanent principle of unity is necessary if the Israelites are to possess their land in peace and enjoy the promises of the Covenant. Thus, the transition from charismatic leader to hereditary kingship is both natural and necessary.

Looking back over the 200-year period we have been speaking about in this chapter, we can only echo the conviction of the author of Joshua: "the Lord God of Israel fought for Israel" (10:42), a phrase that occurs several times throughout the story. The Israelites knew that whenever they obeyed the commands of Moses or Joshua or Gideon, they were really following the beckoning finger of God; Yahweh was their leader, and their successes were due to him. And as we learn more of the history of the orient, we can see, even more clearly than did the harassed Israelites, just how effectively Yahweh was fighting for his people. Israel's successful invasion of Canaan was possible because of the peculiar political situation all over the Near East from the thirteenth to the eleventh century B.C. Egypt, which in an earlier age, would have repulsed any such attempt on Canaan, had fallen into disarray, hopelessly split into a northern and southern kingdom. In Mesopotamia no great power had either the desire or the capacity to dispute possession of Canaan. At that time, Assyria's territory had dwindled, and it was no longer able to defend, much less extend, its borders. There is no exaggeration but only realism in the phrase of Joshua 24:17-18: "for it is the Lord our God who brought us and our fathers up from the land of Egypt, out of the house of bondage, and who did those great signs in our sight, and preserved us in all the way that we went, and among all the peoples through whom we passed; and the Lord drove out before us all the peoples, the Amorites who lived in the land; therefore we also will serve the Lord, for he is our God."

CHAPTER 7

The Kingdom of David

Reading: 1 Samuel 1—2 Samuel 22
1 Kings 1—2 Kings 23
1 Chronicles, chapters 10–25
2 Chronicles, chapters 1–35
Ecclesiasticus, chapter 47

THE story of the royal house of David extends over six books of the Old Testament, the books of Samuel, Kings and Chronicles. The kingdom of David is a historical link that joins Old Testament and New into one continuous unbroken chain of salvation history. This is the meaning of the opening chapter of the New Testament, Matthew 1, which traces the finger of God through history from Abraham to Christ. Matthew 1:1 states this union between the two Testaments aptly: "The book of the genealogy of Jesus Christ, the son of David, the son of Abraham." So, in talking about the kingdom of David, we shall do more than study a few chapters of ancient Palestinian history; we shall see how God used the experiences of this era to prepare men's minds for the coming of a greater king and the accomplishing of our salvation. The kingdom of David is the gateway into the kingdom of God.

Although all Old Testament royalty is associated with the name of David, he was neither the first nor the only king of the Israelites, and in this chapter we shall try to look at the whole period of the kings. That means that we shall be dealing with the period from the crowning of the first king, Saul, about 1020, to the humiliation of the last king of Judah, Zedekiah, in 586 B.C. This period of about 450 years falls naturally into three sections:

1. A single kingdom—under Saul, David, Solomon—lasting about 100 years, whose dominant note is splendour.
2. Two kingdoms—from the death of Solomon to the fall of the northern kingdom in 722—about 200 years, mostly of internal strife.
3. Kingdom of Judah alone—from 722 to 586 (i.e. 135 years), and they were years of slow decay.

Samuel

As we pass from the period of the Judges to that of the Kings, the outlines of the biblical narrative become easier to follow. Thus, we can move more rapidly through the rest of the story. Also, for this period, we have sufficient information, both from the Bible text and from extra-biblical documents and monuments, to enable us to give, in most cases, certain and accurate dates.

We have seen in the last chapter that the period of the Judges was one of insecurity and uncertainty. The fate of the struggling tribes hung in the balance; their resources were few and their enemies many. It was against this dismal background that Samuel, the last and greatest of the Judges, was born. His birth and youth are described in the first three chapters of 1 Samuel. As you read them, you will notice the resemblances between them and the New Testament account of the birth of John the Baptist. In fact, there is a striking similarity between the career and function of Samuel and John the Baptist. Samuel is the bridge between the era of the Judges and that of the Kings, just as John the Baptist is the bridge between the Old Testament era of promise and the New Testament era of fulfilment. And Samuel points out to the Israelites their first king, just as John will point out the Lamb of God. You will also notice that many phrases from the Canticle of Hannah (1 Sam. 2:1-10) were used by Mary in her Magnificat (Luke 1:46-55). And you will probably agree that chapter three contains the most charming little cameo of Old Testament life—the old and weary priest, the sleeping boy, and the voice of Yahweh.

Samuel grew up to become prophet more than judge, and in his

words the hard-pressed Israelites recognized the authentic call of
Yahweh. He went around from tribe to tribe, attempting to instil a
desire for unity into his compatriots. 1 Samuel 7 emphasizes that
Samuel addressed himself "to all the house of Israel" (v. 3). He
made them aware of the urgent need for unity if they were to
survive and if their covenant with Yahweh was to bear its
promised fruit. As they searched for a principle of national unity
they looked out at the thriving nations around them, and finally
they came to Samuel with their request: ". . . appoint for us a king
to govern us like all the nations" (1 *Sam.* 8:5).

Samuel was taken aback. He knew that Israel needed a single
stable centre of gravity, but was a king the answer to the problem?
Oriental monarchs were despotic and capricious creatures, who
exercised powers of life and death over their subjects. Samuel
warned them: "He will take the tenth of your flocks, and you shall
be his slaves. And in that day you will cry out because of your
king, whom you have chosen for yourselves . . ." (8:17–18).

But, as verse 22 puts it: "And the Lord said to Samuel,
'Hearken to their voice, and make them a king.'" A king they
would have, and whether the Israelites suspected it or not, the
age of kings would bring to Israel its finest hours—and some of its
darkest ones.

1. A Single Kingdom

Saul

The coronation of the first king of Israel is one of the most
delightful stories in the Bible. By nature Saul looked a kingly
figure, and 1 Samuel 9 conveys some of the pride of the Israelites
in their first king. "There was not a man among the people of
Israel more handsome than he; from his shoulders upwards he
was taller than any of the people" (v. 2). But the Bible is never
ashamed to set the simple and the sublime side-by-side, and the
first meeting of Saul and Samuel takes place when Saul is search-
ing for his father's straying donkeys. Samuel first crowned him
secretly, one grey dawn outside the walls of the town, by the age-
old oriental method—anointing with sacred oil. Here you should
read 1 Samuel 9:26–10:1. Later, Samuel presented their new

king publicly to the Israelites: "And Samuel said to all the people, 'Do you see him whom the Lord has chosen? There is none like him among all the people.' And all the people shouted, 'Long live the king!'" (1 *Sam.* 10:24). The date is about 1020 B.C.

Saul's reign began brilliantly, and he routed the enemies of Israel one after another—Ammonites, Philistines, Moabites. It is one of the great tragedies of history that a reign so splendidly begun should end so dismally. But, flushed with his series of successes, Saul grew proud and contemptuous; not content with being king, he made himself priest and prophet as well. In the clamour of battle, the voice of Yahweh grew dim. Finally, Samuel came to him and pronounced the hard saying: "Because you have rejected the word of the Lord, he has also rejected you from being king" (1 *Sam.* 15:23). It was a disappointing beginning to the new kingdom. Saul pleaded with Samuel, and as the old prophet turned to go, Saul pulled at his cloak so violently that a piece of the cloth ripped off in his hand. Samuel pointed to the finger of God even in this: "The Lord has torn the kingdom of Israel from you this day, and has given it to a neighbour of yours, who is better than you" (v. 28). Samuel left, and verse 35 remarks sadly: "And Samuel did not see Saul again until the day of his death, but Samuel grieved over Saul." Samuel set out to find a new king, one who knew how to command men, but also how to obey God.

David

We are introduced to David in 1 Samuel 16–17. These chapters contain three events:

(*a*) Samuel secretly anointed David king. This took place in the house of David's father, Jesse, in Bethlehem of Judah, which Luke 2:4 calls "the city of David". That is why the Roman census sent Joseph down to Bethlehem, "because he was of the house and lineage of David". David was Jesse's youngest son, and up to then had tended sheep. Bethlehem and shepherds seem to be inseparables in the Bible story.

(*b*) The transition from the sheep pastures to Saul's palace is made by the coincidence of David's music and Saul's madness. After his rejection by Samuel, Saul is a depressed and moody man, and even the primitive Israelites knew the therapeutic value of music. "So Saul said to his servants, 'Provide for me a man who can play well, and bring him to me.' One of the young men answered, 'Behold I have seen a son of Jesse the Bethlehemite, who is skilful in playing, a man of valour, a man of war, prudent in speech, and a man of good presence; and the Lord is with him' . . . And David came to Saul and entered his service" (1 *Sam.* 16:17-18; 21). The date is about 1000 B.C.

(*c*) Chapter 17 is a story that has always captivated the imagination of readers—David *v.* Goliath. This incident established David as a hero in the eyes of the Israelites, and 18:7 quotes a line from a "pop song" of the time: "And the women sang to one another as they made merry, 'Saul has slain his thousands, And David his ten thousands.'"

But the sullen Saul grew jealous and violent, and made several attempts on David's life. Eventually David fled from the palace, and thus it happened that he was a fugitive in exile when Saul and his son Jonathan were killed at the battle of Mount Gilboa.

Back came David to claim his throne, and to chant the noblest requiem ever heard over fallen warrior. His love for Jonathan and his forgiveness of Saul combine to give us a poem whose magnificence comes through in any translation. Read it in 2 Samuel 1:19-27.

David had a hard beginning to his royal career. He was not accepted as king by all the twelve tribes until about seven years after Saul's death. The southern tribes of Judah and Benjamin acclaimed him immediately; after all, he was one of their own. But the ten northern tribes were slow to submit to another southerner as king. Finally, they realized that only union under David's leadership could save them from the Philistines, and David's great career really began. He ruled for about forty years, and this reign is described in 2 Samuel 5 — 1 Kings 2, part of which was probably the first section of the Old Testament to be put in writing—soon after David's death. This is the very stuff of history—vivid description, honest reporting, and the rich colours of the oriental story-teller. Nobody should abstain from the joy of reading it.

We can mention only a few of the landmarks in that narrative.

(a) *Definitive defeat of the Philistines:* These sea-coast dwellers had always been a thorn in the side of the Israelites. They had invaded Palestine from the sea about the same time as Joshua had crossed the Jordan, and had established a "kingdom" of five cities in the south-western corner of the country, by the sea. They harrassed the Israelites all during the era of the Judges, and their name is associated in the Bible with all that is most detestable in paganism. Thus the word "philistine" has come into English idiom to denote an uncouth and uncultured man or manner. David not alone pushed them back out of Israelite territory, but almost pushed them into the sea. By a strange twist of fate, the Philistines were destined to give its modern name to the Israelite territory; the word "Palestine" is merely a corruption of "Philistine".

(b) *Capture of Jerusalem:* This Canaanite fortress-city, Jebus, on a rocky peak in the Judean hills, had resisted many Israelite attacks since the time of Joshua. It was unusually well-situated from the military point of view—overlooking the surrounding valleys and approaches. David captured Jerusalem, and decided to make it his capital. And now it too is called the city of David. The choice of Jerusalem as capital was a wise one, for two reasons. First, its position enabled it to be defended nobly against an enemy assault, which often happened afterwards; secondly, it stood almost on the border between the land of Judah and that of the northern tribes, and David felt that having the royal residence here would make his rule more acceptable to the northern group.

(c) *Jerusalem as Religious Centre:* The pagan Canaanites had local deities, each city having a temple to its own particular god. Since Israel worshipped one God, David decreed that there be only one temple, to avoid the danger of imitating the pagan territorial deities. Therefore he brought the Ark of the Covenant in triumph to Jerusalem—and the city of David became the city of God, the holy city. His great desire was to build a temple in Jerusalem to house the Ark, but this was not to be; his son would build it. But David did adapt the ritual of the desert Tabernacle to the new permanent conditions, and laid the groundwork for the temple liturgy that would continue all through the Old Testament. For example, he divided the priests into twenty-four teams, to function in weekly rotation. This is what is referred to in Luke 1:8-9 about the priest Zechariah. "Now while he was serving as priest before God when his division was on duty, according to the customs of the priesthood . . ." David also appointed levites to supervise public ceremonies and to lead the community chants, and this is the origin of a nucleus of the Psalter.

The Bible is a delightfully realistic book, and side-by-side with the glories of David it records faithfully the decline of his latter years. The story of his passion for Bathsheba is so well known that we need only mention it. With cold-blooded calculation he arranged for her husband's death in battle. There follows, in 2 Samuel 12, one of the liveliest pieces of writing in the Old Testament—the dramatic confrontation of King David and the prophet Nathan. Please read vv. 1-25.

Nathan's threat was amply executed; David did encounter much evil out of his own house. His son Absalom hatched a conspiracy against him, secretly enlisted the aid of some of the northern tribes against the king, and David had to flee Jerusalem. 2 Samuel 15 chronicles the sorry journey of the ageing and broken-hearted king driven from his royal city, crossing the brook Kidron and going up the Mount of Olives—the route of another sad journey one thousand years later. "But David went up the ascent of the Mount of Olives, weeping as he went, barefoot and with his head covered; and all the people who were with him covered their heads, and they went up, weeping as they went" (15:30).

David endured many humiliations, and paid dearly for his faults, before the revolt was finally crushed and he could return to his palace. But David was magnanimous, big in heart and mind. He wept for the death of his rebellious son Absalom as he had wept for his persecutor Saul: "O my son Absalom, my son, my son Absalom! Would I had died instead of you, O Absalom, my son, my son!" (18:33). And his repentance for his sins was great and public, forming the basis of our Psalm 51, the Miserere.

Among the cruel and sensual oriental kings of the time, David stands out as a noble figure, whose long and turbulent life was spent in active devotion to the cause of Yahweh. And to him and his descendants the prophet Nathan relayed God's promise: "And your house and your kingdom shall be made sure for ever before me; your throne shall be established for ever" (2 Sam. 7:16). The dynasty of David continued in Jerusalem through fair times and foul. Many of his successors were weak and wicked, and in the sad days pious Israelites looked back with pride and longing to the era of David, the hero-king. And when they spoke of the hoped-for Messiah, they thought of him as another David, one who would restore glory and honour to the royal house of the shepherd-boy from Bethlehem. And it is in these terms that Gabriel announced the birth of Christ to Mary: "He will be great, and will be called the Son of the Most High; and the Lord God will give to him the throne of his father David, and he will reign over the house of Jacob for ever; and of his kingdom there will be no end" (*Luke* 1:32–3). And when the enthusiastic crowd swirls around Christ on Palm Sunday they shout: "Hosanna to the Son of David!"

Solomon

David's military successes gave Israel peace and prosperity, and so his son Solomon was able to devote all his energies to internal organization. He was the only king in Old Testament history who never had to wage a war, even though he reigned for forty years—approximately 961–922 B.C. These forty years can be summed up in two words: magnificence and wealth. This period was, in human terms, the pinnacle of Israel's glory.

Solomon's most striking single achievement was the *building of the Temple* at Jerusalem. 1 Kings describes it in detail, and it must have been one of the finest buildings in the world of the time.

Solomon imported the choicest materials in timber and stone, sending north to Lebanon for cedarwood—and craftsmen. This temple took seven years to build, and it was opened with a solemn dedication ceremony of public prayer and sacrifice. Read all about it in 1 Kings 8.

Solomon was the first to establish *commercial relations* between Israel and the surrounding nations. He built a fleet of ships, which carried to Israel the costliest luxuries of the ancient world; as 1 Kings 10:22 puts it: "Once every three years the fleet of ships of Tarshish used to come bringing gold, silver, ivory, apes, and peacocks."

This is the verse that provided John Masefield with the idea for his poem "Cargoes":

> Quinquireme of Nineveh from distant Ophir
> Rowing home to haven in sunny Palestine,
> With a cargo of ivory,
> And apes and peacocks,
> Sandalwood, cedarwood, and sweet white wine.

Solomon also established *diplomatic relations* with the neighbouring empires, and Jerusalem witnessed the spectacle of royal visitors coming to admire the work and wisdom of Solomon. Israel had finally taken her place among the nations of the earth; the Israelites had come a long way from the desert tents. Christ was using a commonplace image when he said: " . . . even Solomon in all his glory was not arrayed like one of these" (*Matt.* 6:29).

But even these few examples of Solomon's achievements show that his ambitions were worldly ones, and the fact emerges that he was too engrossed in material splendour to be deeply religious. He did spend seven years building the temple, but he spent thirteen years building his royal palaces. His matrimonial affairs were on the same grand scale; in this sphere also he vied with his fellow-kings of the orient. 1 Kings 11 gives the statistics: "Now King Solomon loved many foreign women . . . He had seven hundred wives, princesses, and three hundred concubines; and his wives turned away his heart" (vv. 1;3). It indicates the results: "For when Solomon was old his wives turned away his heart after other gods; and his heart was not wholly true to the Lord his God, as was the heart of David his father" (v. 4). It announces the punishment: "Therefore the Lord said to Solomon, 'Since this has been your mind and you have not kept my covenant and my statutes which I have commanded you, I will surely tear the kingdom from you and will give it to your servant. Yet for the sake of David your father I will not do it in your days, but I will tear it out of the hand of your son' " (v. 11–12). And that is how, politically speaking, Israel's golden age led her straight to disaster.

2. The Divided Kingdom

The division came immediately on the death of Solomon. His son, Rehoboam, succeeded him. In his first meeting with the northern tribes, Rehoboam's ill-advised adolescent arrogance so antagonized them that they promptly refused allegiance. 1 Kings 12 reports the interview graphically. A northerner, Jeroboam, had led an abortive revolt against Solomon and had fled to Egypt for safety. Now he returns to be leader and spokesman of the northern tribes. The rebel and the young king face one another. Rehoboam rejects a reasonable request with scorn: "And now, whereas my father laid upon you a heavy yoke, I will add to your yoke. My father chastised you with whips, but I will chastise you with scorpions" (v. 11).

The real causes of the division, however, were deeper. The seeds of dissension had always been there; we have seen the reluctance of the northern bloc to accept David as king. Rehoboam's tactlessness provided the occasion for the final rift. Also, Solomon's magnificence was an expensive luxury. The cost of his ambitious building projects, of his army, of his court life, had to be borne by taxation, and also by forced labour. This was precisely Jeroboam's complaint. Throughout Solomon's reign the progressively sharper contrast between the royal extravagance and the people's poverty had bred deep social unrest.

There were other reasons for the division, but we have said

enough to show that, as one writer remarks, Solomon at his death could well have used the phrase of another monarch: "After me —the deluge." The deluge came, and the Israelites never again became a united people.

The results of the split were political and religious schism.

Political Schism

The boundary between the two kingdoms ran from the northern tip of the Dead Sea to Joppa on the coast, thus dividing Palestine into two independent kingdoms of unequal size. The southern one, comprising Judah and Benjamin, took the name Judah and continued to be ruled by the dynasty of David. The northern one elected Jeroboam as its first king, and took the proud name Israel, because it included ten of the twelve tribes. It is also referred to as Ephraim, from the border tribe. It had a larger territory and more numerous population than Judah, but lacked internal unity and was more exposed to attack from surrounding empires.

Religious Schism

Since the Bible is a theology of history rather than a textbook of history, it presents the religious schism as the real tragedy of the divided kingdom. Just as religious zeal for their common Yahweh had welded the groups into a unit in the days of the desert and Sinai, so now their internal bickering was a symptom of an abandonment of Yahweh, the true God. David and Solomon had made Jerusalem a pivotal centre of religious worship, and this unity of sanctuary helped to foster their wavering unity of kingdom. Now the temple at Jerusalem was in the hands of Judah, and the northern kingdom set up rival sanctuaries at Dan and Bethel. The Jerusalem temple contained their most sacred object, the Ark of the Covenant, and so the northern sanctuaries created sacred objects of their own—in the dangerous form of golden calves. Thus began the downward path to the gross idolatry that the prophets were later to denounce.

As a political expedient, partition has rarely been a success, and in the case of Palestine the partition of the kingdom led to two hundred years of hostility, distrust and occasionally open and cruel civil war. The story is the same in both kingdoms—each has a long line of undistinguished and sometimes evil rulers. The situation was particularly lamentable in Israel, where political intrigue produced nineteen kings in two hundred years. Of the four kings who immediately succeeded Jeroboam, only one enjoyed the luxury of a natural death; one committed suicide after seven days on the throne, and two were murdered after a two-year reign. Only one of Israel's kings seems to have ruled with strength and skill—Omri, who built a new city, Samaria, to be his capital, and made an alliance between the two kingdoms. But even Omri gained the crown by a military coup d'état, and the dynasty he founded came to a violent end in a cruel blood-bath in 843 B.C.

It is not difficult to see why this unhappy kingdom fell an easy prey to the Assyrian army that laid siege to Samaria in 725. Surprisingly, the city held out for three years. In 722 it was captured by the Assyrian king, Sargon II, whose first act was to uproot and deport nearly 30,000 Israelites. In this way, the ten northern tribes stumbled into oblivion, never to be heard of again. They were never again assembled into one territory, and so they have been called the ten lost tribes of Israel. The Assyrians planted Samaria with the deportees from other conquered countries like Arabia and Babylon, and these pagan foreigners settled down to live and marry with the few Israelites left behind. The resultant population, hybrid in race and religion, formed the Samaritan race, which we shall meet again, in both Old and New Testaments, as a group hated by and hostile to the true sons of Abraham.

3. Kingdom of Judah alone

The tiny kingdom of Judah now stands alone, an insignificant island in an ocean of powerful pagan empires. This defenceless kingdom survived for 135 years. It had two good kings. Hezechiah (about 700 B.C.) paid tribute to Assyria, and as a result was left in peace. This peace he employed to institute a genuine religious reform. About eighty years later, a great-grandson of Hezechiah, Josiah, found himself on the throne of Judah at the age of eight. He grew up to be the greatest of Judah's kings, and 2 Chronicles 34:2-3 say of him: "He did what was right in the eyes of the Lord, and walked in the ways of David his father; and he did not turn aside to the right or to the left. For in the eighth year of his reign, while he was yet a boy, he began to seek the God of David his father."

He set on foot a renovation of the temple, and during this project the high priest found what the Bible calls "the book of the law of Yahweh", containing some of our Book of Deuteronomy. Josiah ordered the "law of Yahweh" read aloud, and shocked Judah into a realization of its sinfulness. On the crest of this renewed zeal, and aided by the prophet Jeremiah, Josiah launched a radical religious reform, ordered all Israelites to Jerusalem to celebrate the Pasch, and renewed the ancient covenant with Yahweh. During his reign, a little of the old Davidic splendour glowed briefly; it was the last gleam of glory before the long night descended.

Away to the north-east, Assyria was crumbling, and the new empire of Babylon was spreading. To the south, Egypt viewed the rise of Babylon with alarm, and finally decided to march north in support of the dying Assyrian empire. Marching north meant marching through Judah, and Josiah, in his last heroic but imprudent gesture, faced the Egyptian army in the battle of Megiddo in 609 B.C. Josiah was killed and Judah defeated. It was the beginning of the end, and nothing could now save Judah from the fate of her sister-kingdom. At this point we can pause for the present; and at this point we shall take up the story again when we come to talk about the fall of Jerusalem and the Babylonian captivity.

History and Salvation History

Now, as we glance back at this long list of names and dates, of human failings and political intrigues, we must face the question: What does it all mean? In what way does this piece of history differ from the human history of any war-torn country? How does it claim to be a chapter of salvation history? These are profound questions, and we can present only an outline of the answer.

(a) The Old Testament authors set out to relate the interventions of Yahweh in Israel's history, and Israel's response to Yahweh's interventions. Their selection of material, and their manner of presenting it, were governed by this aim. Their view of their own history is this: how God called Israel to be his people; how Israel responded to his call; how, despite his people's infidelity, God, "the Hound of Heaven", pursued them with divine affection; how eventually he would lead them, in his good time, to the fulfilment of their destiny. Thus, in the story of the Davidic dynasty, the author's purpose is to present its establishment as a divine intervention, and its permanence as a divine promise. And in 1 and 2 Kings, the purpose is to show how the division and the ultimate fall of the kingdom resulted, not from God's forgetfulness of his covenant, but from the kings' infidelity to it.

(b) Salvation history is the story of God at work in the world of men. Yahweh's covenant with Israel created salvation history. By that act, God took the destiny of humans in hand and began to guide their course towards a goal that he alone knew. From this moment on, the sequence of historical events has acquired a meaning; it now traces a pattern that is governed by a divine idea, a master-plan.

(c) This first intervention of God, in the exodus and the covenant, was a saving act, a salvation act, and that is why we speak of "salvation history". Before Israel knew anything else about God, she knew him to be a saving God. And he continued to be a saving God. Israel knew, then, that the destination towards which he was guiding her was a salvation, an ultimate saving. But Israel learned only slowly and painfully what form this final saving would take. At first, the Israelites felt that salvation would be theirs in the possession of the Promised Land. But life under Joshua and the Judges was still perilous. Then they

8

looked for salvation in a kingdom, but we have seen how Israel's dream of a material kingdom of God was shattered again and again. But God was still a saving God, and, while mighty empires crashed about her, Israel survived and struggled on. And Israel's hope of a final salvation lived on.

(*d*) With the prophets, this hope took the form of a yearning for another and greater David, who would bring to perfection all that Yahweh had promised to the house of David. In this way, God used the fragments of Israel's shattered dreams to create a vision of the Messiah-King, whose throne would be universal and eternal. And thus the ancient kingdom of David, for all its failings, pointed the way to Christ, through whose saving death we have all become members of what St Peter called "a chosen race, a royal priesthood" (*1 Pet.* 2:9).

CHAPTER 8

The Prophets of Israel and Judah

Reading: 1 Kings, chapter 13
1 Kings, 17—2 Kings 2
Amos, chapters 1–8
Ecclesiasticus, chapters 48–9

IN the last chapter we followed the fortunes of the Old Testament kings through their glorious days and their gloomy ones. We saw that originally a king was the Israelites' idea, and we saw too that it was not a very successful experiment. Now we turn to a different institution in Israel, one that was God's idea, namely prophecy. The Israelites neither asked for nor appointed the prophets. The prophets were called by God, and they are the great figures that shed lustre on the tottering kingdoms of Israel and Judah. But then—the prophets were God's idea, not Israel's. While other nations revere their kings and warriors as their national heroes, Israel's greatest men are her prophets. It was they who sustained her in the storm, and it is not surprising that, when Israel finally assembled her sacred writings, our Old Testament, one-third of the total should be prophecy.

The Historical Setting of the Prophets

There is another reason for turning immediately from kings to prophets, namely, it is precisely during the period of the kings that the great age of prophecy begins in Israel. There had always been prophets in Israel's history, but the age of the writing prophets, prophets whose sermons have been transmitted to us in the Bible, is a sharply delimited period—from the eighth to the fourth century B.C. The first of the writing prophets, Amos, appeared about 150 years after the partition of the kingdom. Prophecy continued during the remaining half-century of hostility between Israel and Judah, continued while Judah stood alone, continued during the exile, and continued during the hard and disappointing years after the return to Jerusalem, when many of the people grew disillusioned and apathetic. The gift of prophecy seems to have faded out gently in the fourth century; there is no further prophet until John the Baptist, the final herald of the Messiah and the greatest prophet of them all. This means that prophecy flourished precisely during Israel's darkest and most dangerous years; it seems to have been God's providential aid to his people in distress.

Chronologically, we speak of the prophets in terms of three periods, according to their relation to the Babylonian exile in the sixth century.

1. *Pre-exilic prophets*, e.g. Amos, Hosea, Micah, Isaiah (chapters 1–35), Jeremiah.

2. *Prophets of the exile*, i.e. Ezekiel, Deutero-Isaiah (chapters 40–45). We shall explain the term Deutero-Isaiah in the next chapter.

3. *Post-exilic prophets*, e.g. Zechariah, Malachi.

Of course, we are speaking here only of the writing prophets. But many of the great prophets of Israel left no body of writing behind them, and we know of their activity only from the historical books. For an interesting view of prophecy in the early days of the kings, see 1 Kings 13. Outstanding examples of non-writing prophets are Elijah, Elisha, Nathan. The career of Elijah is typical, and it is described in a section we have already seen, 1 Kings 17—2 Kings 2. These men were true prophets, and they exercised a profound influence on the history and religious thought of Israel. They enjoyed prophetic inspiration, but not biblical inspiration, that is they were not moved by God to set down his message in writing.

The Nature of Prophecy

In modern English the word "prophecy" suggests chiefly the foretelling of future events. But this is not exactly the Old Testament sense of the word "prophet".

Our word "prophet" comes from the Greek "pro-phetes", which means: speaking for, on behalf of, another. In the Old Testament context, then, it means one who speaks to men for God, on behalf of God. A prophet is a messenger of God, announcing the divine will, a spokesman for Yahweh in the rough and tumble of daily life in Israel. This is why the Old Testament applies the word to most of its great figures, such as Abraham, Moses, Samuel. And in the New Testament St Matthew reports how the Jerusalem crowds spoke of Christ on Palm Sunday: "And the crowds said, 'This is the prophet Jesus from Nazareth of Galilee.'" (21:11).

The prophets were primarily preachers, preachers whose only claim to a hearing was that their preaching was not their own but God's. The Bible uses the simple phrase: "the word of the Lord came to" (Jeremiah, Isaiah, etc.) to describe the prophetic activity; in fact, the Bible's definition of a prophet is: a man to whom "the word of the Lord came". And that is almost the only common factor among the prophets of Israel and Judah; otherwise they differ vastly from one another—in education, in experience, in preaching emphasis. Amos was a shepherd, Isaiah a palace adviser—Foreign Secretary to kings, Ezekiel a priest. Prophecy was not an hereditary function; there never was a house of prophecy as there was a house of kings. And prophecy was not restricted to a particular tribe or family, as Israelite priesthood was restricted to the tribe of Levi. Each prophet was personally called by God, and sent to carry God's words to his people.

A prophet, then, was sent to his contemporaries. His preaching was of the present and to his immediate audience. It was intended to move them, to warn them of approaching punishment for their sinfulness, to console them with the hope of a great deliverer to come. Therefore each prophet was primarily concerned with the present, and it was not his function to provide a timetable of future events. Most of the prophets did make statements concerning the future, but these were made only because that future had a relation to the present; for instance, they foretold future punishment in an attempt to convert their present audience; they foretold the future Messiah in order to sustain and console the dispirited Israelites of the evil days. Also, their vision of the future was limited and partial. They were not granted a cinematic preview of coming events. They foresaw dimly, and much of the time their hearers only partially understood. In essence, their function was to announce the wishes of Yahweh—to tell forth rather than to foretell.

Because they were preachers, men who stood at the temple gates or in the city streets and yelled at the top of their voices "the word of the Lord", their words do not come to us in quite the same style as the other books of the Old Testament. They all preached before they wrote; in most cases, their preaching was written down and edited later by their disciples. Because they were preachers, their chief aim was to move an audience to action. They did not offer arguments or proofs; they presented God as a just God, a loving God, an almighty God, and they flung his holiness in the face of the people. Again, because they were preachers they used all the tricks of the preacher's trade—flights of oratory, parables, paradoxes and puns. They exhorted, threatened, coaxed—and insulted their hearers. They stormed the will with a torrent of words and images, and often they underlined their words with dramatic gestures and symbolic actions. For example, chapter 19 of Jeremiah tells how he took an earthenware water-jar, and commanded the priests and the chief citizens of Jerusalem to accompany him outside the city gate down into the valley of Hinnom. This was part of his prophetic inspiration, and so he writes it all down as the word of the Lord. "Then you shall break the flask in the sight of the men who go with you, and shall say to them, 'Thus says the Lord of hosts: So will I break this people and this city, as one breaks a potter's vessel, so that it can never be mended.'" (vv. 10–11).

The prophets preached nothing radical or revolutionary. Rather, they tried to recall Israel to the old themes and the old truths—to the memory of the exodus and God's guiding care in the desert, to Sinai and the Decalogue, to the early days when Yahweh was their God but they were really his people. They pointed out how far Israel had wandered from her historical mission as the people of Yahweh, and they denounced the sinfulness of their own times, the idolatry, the injustice and the empty self-righteousness of the splintered kingdom.

False Prophets

Of course, there were false prophets and pagan prophets, men who pretended to speak the words of God but who had received no divine commission to do so. False prophets tended to attach themselves to a wealthy man or to a king, and they made sure to present him with oracles suited to his ambitions and the prevailing condition of his liver. Micah, who preached in the eighth century, complained bitterly about these flatterers and their soothsaying. This is how he describes them:

> . . . who cry 'Peace'
> when they have something to eat,
> but declare war against him
> who puts nothing into their mouths (3:5).

He goes on to say that they

> . . . divine for money;
> yet they lean upon the Lord and say,
> 'Is not the Lord in the midst of us?
> No evil shall come upon us' (3:11).

And there were pagan prophets—a bizarre mixture of fortune-tellers, magicians and faith-healers who plied their trade all over the ancient world, as far as historical records show. In Palestine, these claimed to be the prophets of Baal, the god par excellence of the Palestinian pagans. These were always a thorn in the side of the prophets of Yahweh, and on one great occasion there is a dramatic contest between them, when one true prophet of the true God challenges hundreds of the false prophets of Baal—and

emerges triumphant. It makes great reading, and it is found in
1 Kings 18. Elijah, stout-hearted defender of Yahweh in the
difficult days of King Ahab, defended his right to preach by
throwing down a challenge: let all the prophets of Baal meet him
on the top of Mount Carmel, that lovely hill overlooking the Bay
of Haifa, and there, in public, Elijah would prove his case. He
would prove, not that he was greater than they, but that his God
was greater than Baal. 1 Kings 18 is well worth reading.

The prophets of Israel, then, were men of God, and men who
relayed to their fellows the words of God. This they did, and
could do, because: (a) each had been *called* personally by God;
(b) each had been *sent* by God to a definite audience and with a
definite message. These two aspects, being called by God and
being sent by God, gave the prophets their unique status, and so
we should look a little more closely at these two facts. It is useless
to pretend that we shall understand fully the nature of the
prophetic vocation and prophetic mission; these are divine actions
deep in a man's soul, and an element of mystery must ever
remain about them.

Prophetic Vocation

What the Epistle to the Hebrews says of the priesthood is
equally applicable to the office of prophet: "one does not take the
honour upon himself" (5:4). A prophet's only justification for
preaching was that he had been called personally by God to be a
prophet. When the priest of the Bethel temple ordered Amos to go
home and preach to his own people, Amos' only reply—and
adequate reply—was: ". . . the Lord took me from following the
flock, and the Lord said to me, 'Go, prophesy to my people
Israel.' Now therefore hear the word of the Lord . . ." (*Amos*
7:15–16).

Normally, the prophet's call took the form of an inner invitation, an invitation that had as its basis some external event or
object. And this call was the influence that moulded the prophet's
whole career and determined his specific way of seeing things—
and of preaching things. Usually, the prophets relate it in terms

of a vision. For example, Isaiah tells us of his vocation in chapter 6. He describes how he saw the Lord enthroned in glory, angels adoring him with the cry: "Holy, holy, holy is the Lord of hosts; the whole earth is full of his glory."

The area all about was filled with smoke, and Isaiah became aware of his unworthiness: "Woe is me! For I am lost; for I am a man of unclean lips . . ." An angel took a burning coal from an altar fire and touched his lips. "And I heard the voice of the Lord saying, 'Whom shall I send, and who will go for us?' Then I said, 'Here I am! Send me!'" (v. 8).

What are we to make of all this? It is hardly necessary to presume that it is exclusively a vision, a private revelation in which Isaiah is shown Yahweh enthroned in heaven. This could, of course, be the case. But there is a possible alternative, and that is that God made use of a perfectly normal event in the man's life in order to illuminate his mind and urge him into the prophetic office. The description given by Isaiah savours of the Jerusalem temple on a feast day. The Ark of the Covenant is there, in the Holy of Holies, surmounted by the cherubim, and this place the Israelites regarded as the presence of God in their midst. Worshippers thronged the temple, singing psalms and praying aloud. The smoke from the sacrifices filled the air. Isaiah is there, visiting the temple, perhaps a routine visit of a pious Israelite. But God seizes this occasion to open the eyes of Isaiah —to flood his mind with a divine illumination by which Isaiah sees above and beyond the temple to the real throne of God, sees beyond the temple worshippers to the adoring angels at Yahweh's throne, sees beyond the psalms of the pilgrims to the angels' ceaseless worship of God's unspeakable sanctity. Isaiah becomes aware, for the first time, of his own great unworthiness face-to-face with God's great holiness, and driven by this conviction he offers himself as a mouthpiece of God's holiness to the sinful people of Judah. This awareness of the holiness of God remained the dominant idea in Isaiah's life and preaching. It is only natural that a man's first striking contact with God should colour his whole life and thought. St Paul is a splendid example of this. On the Damascus road Christ had asked him abruptly:

why do you persecute me? The union between Christ and his followers implied in this question so burned itself into Paul's mind that it became his master idea, and he spent the remainder of his life preaching the reality of the Mystical Body. With Isaiah, too, God becomes, and remains, "the Holy One of Israel". God had done more than touch his lips with a burning coal; he had touched his soul with a blinding revelation—and Isaiah set out on a long career of preaching the sanctity of God and the sinfulness of men.

Jeremiah tells us of two visions that orientated his prophetic career. But, whereas Isaiah had volunteered for the privilege, Jeremiah was a reluctant prophet. He was honourable, and ready to do Yahweh's will, but he was a timid and sensitive young man, a quiet country boy, probably in his twenties, when God called him. Anxiously, he asked God to find somebody else, to let the chalice pass from him:

"Ah, Lord God! Behold, I do not know how to speak,
for I am only a youth." But the Lord said to me,
"Do not say, 'I am only a youth';
for to all to whom I send you you shall go,
and whatever I command you you shall speak.
Be not afraid of them,
for I am with you to deliver you, says the Lord."
(*Jer.* 1:6–8)

Then God uses two little visions to enlighten Jeremiah, and you will find them described in 1:11–15. These seem to be simple domestic incidents from the young man's daily life. High in the Judean hills he admires the almond tree, the first plant in Palestine to bloom in the springtime. In Hebrew it was called "shaqed"—and the verb "to watch" is "shaqad". Jeremiah must have grinned a little uneasily as the divine pun struck him! And another day, as he squatted beside the fire waiting for a pot to boil, he noticed that it hung in a lopsided way from the hook, leaning away from the northern hills of Ephraim on the horizon. And this simple accident became, by divine illumination, an arrow pointing out the direction from which Judah's humiliation would come. This enemy from the north never left Jeremiah's thought — until at last the enemy from the north burst through the walls of Jerusalem in 586 B.C. and the Babylonian captivity began. Jeremiah was the only prophet crying out "in the hearing of Jerusalem" at its fall; as he watched the sack of the city did he recall the day that a pot almost fell into the fire?

Perhaps the most extraordinary vocation of all was that by which Hosea became a prophet. The first three chapters of the book of Hosea have always tantalized readers, but the following seems a reasonable interpretation of them. Hosea was a good man whose marriage turned out an unhappy one. Having borne him three children, his wife Gomer took up, not with another man, but with a number of men. Hosea divorced her according to the Mosaic law, and she apparently became a temple prostitute in one of the pagan shrines of the northern kingdom. In the eyes of a pious Israelite—and Hosea was one—this was the lowest any girl could go. But Hosea's life and actions are dominated by Yahweh, and so Hosea takes her back, in fact, ransoms her from the pagan shrine—"bought her for fifteen shekels of silver" (3:2). And he goes on to say (v. 5): "Afterwards the children of Israel shall return and seek the Lord their God . . ." In other words, God enlightens Hosea and enables him to see in his painful domestic tragedy a picture of the infidelity of Israel. Israel had been espoused to Yahweh—this is what the Sinai covenant meant for the prophets. But she proved an unfaithful spouse who turned her back on Yahweh to worship false gods. This idolatry the prophets always called adultery. As Jeremiah says bluntly: "Have you seen what she did, that faithless one, Israel, how she went up on every high hill and under every green tree, and there played the harlot?" (3:6).

Hosea saw that his own generous action in taking back Gomer mirrored, however faintly, the patience of a loving God who will forgive and finally restore erring Israel. And Hosea preached the mercy and tenderness of God so insistently that he has become known as the prophet of divine love. This is how he expresses the love of Yahweh for Israel:

> When Israel was a child, I loved him,
> and out of Egypt I called my son . . .
> Yet it was I who taught Ephraim to walk,
> I took them up in my arms;
> but they did not know that I healed them (11:1; 3).

Prophetic Mission

The prophets were called by God. They were also sent by God —to a specific milieu in definite historical circumstances. The gift of prophecy was not given to them for their own benefit—it was given for the benefit of their audiences. This prophetic commission often led them to a hostile audience, uncongenial surroundings and a life of hardship. Perhaps we tend to think of the prophets as remote mystics, serene contemplatives who spoke with God, far removed from the heat and dust of the market-place. But none of the Old Testament prophets was quite like that. They were all plunged into the bustle and turmoil of a chaotic period in their nation's history, they were caught up in all the religious and political tensions of their day. They were public figures, and their function was to proclaim aloud the word of Yahweh, as Jeremiah puts it, "against the kings of Judah, its princes, its priests, and the people of the land" (1:18). They were men of the spirit, but they were also men of the world—in the good sense.

Some of them were actively involved in the political life of their time, and much of their preaching originally took the form of advice, reproof, warning to the reigning king. For example, Isaiah served as adviser to a succession of kings of Judah, and strove to convince them of the hopelessness of trusting in Egypt rather than in Yahweh. Jeremiah had the unpopular task of urging king and people to surrender to the Babylonians, and was imprisoned and reviled as a traitor. But, while the preaching and the advice of the prophets were often ignored, they did give to the nation what armies or diplomacy could not give—the conviction that, in spite of disaster and defeat, Israel was still, and would remain, the People of God.

When a prophet was sent by God to preach, he was sent on a difficult and often dangerous mission. The prophets suffered much. They suffered because they had to pronounce the punishment of God on their fellow-Israelites and their native land. They suffered because they tried heroically to wean their people from idolatry and its chastisement, but had to watch helplessly as king and people obstinately went their way to destruction. Micah expressed how he felt:

> For this I will lament and wail;
> I will go stripped and naked;
> I will make lamentation like the jackals,
> and mourning like the ostriches.
> For her wound is incurable;
> and it has come to Judah,
> it has reached to the gate of my people,
> to Jerusalem (1:8-9).

The prophets encountered opposition and persecution from kings and court officials. And no one more than Jeremiah, the shy young man from the village of Anathoth. All the citizens of Jerusalem conspire against him—Jeremiah 18; he is put in the stocks to be jeered at publicly, in chapter 20; he is imprisoned, in chapter 37; he is thrown down a well and left to die a slow death (until a slave rescues him)—chapter 38. Small wonder that he once cried out in exasperation:

> Cursed be the day
> on which I was born!
> The day when my mother bore me,
> let it not be blessed!
> Cursed be the man
> who brought the news to my father,
> "A son is born to you,"
> making him very glad (*Jer.* 20:14-15).

Prophecies of Hope

If one were to read only sections of the writings of the prophets, one could come away with the impression that they were professional prophets of doom, that the theme of their preaching was unremitted disaster—dungeon, fire and sword upon the whole Near East. They foretell the punishment of Israel by her powerful pagan neighbours, and in turn foretell the ultimate collapse of these great empires. But it is a mistake to read only a section of any prophetical book; we should read all of it. And then we shall see that there is always a ray of hope in the surrounding gloom of their predictions. This ray of hope takes three chief forms, all of them facets of the same central truth: (i) the survival of a chosen group, a purified "remnant" of Israel; (ii) the coming of a triumphant liberator, a Messiah; (iii) the universality of the salvation that this Messiah will bring—he will be liberator, not merely of Israel, but of all humanity.

The "remnant" idea is one of the most constant prophetic themes of consolation. This remnant, a devoted minority of survivors, will be the channel of Yahweh's blessing; through this remnant the promises of the covenant will be transmitted, the torch will be passed on until it blaze finally into the glory of the Messiah. And in this idea of remnant we have the first faint glimpse of a chosen society, purified by suffering, that will be a leaven among the nations. This concept was the gentle preparation of human minds for the mystery of Christ's Church in the world.

The two other related ideas, a personal Messiah, bringing universal salvation, we shall see expressed in their most eloquent form in the prophets of the exile, especially in Deutero-Isaiah.

The Book of Amos

In making the acquaintance of the prophets for the first time, it is probably best to begin with one of the shorter books. We may take the Book of Amos as an example. It contains only nine short chapters, its structure is typical of that of most of the others, and, as we said already, Amos was the first, or one of the first, of the writing prophets.

Amos is introduced in 1:1 as being from "among the shepherds of Tekoa", a little village south of Bethlehem. Memories and metaphors from his shepherd days in the poor pastures of southern Judah crowd upon us as we read the fiery speeches of his later prophetic ministry—the loneliness of the semi-desert, the hazards from wild beasts and bandits, the cart groaning under the corn, etc. His prophetic mission was not to his own Judah, but to the northern kingdom of Israel, about thirty or forty years before its defeat and disappearance. Accustomed to the poverty and hardship of the shepherd's life, he is shocked into anger by the ill-gotten and ill-spent riches of the northern cities, where people "lie upon beds of ivory", and "anoint themselves with the finest oils, but are not grieved over the ruin of Joseph!" (*Amos* 6).

Perhaps we come closer to the correct chronological order if we re-arrange the text thus:

(*a*) Chapters 7–8: A series of visions, which probably give us the prophetic vocation of Amos.

(*b*) Chapter 1: His first sermon or sermons, foretelling approaching disaster on all Israel's enemies. This news would have fallen like sweet music on the ears of his audience in Bethel or Samaria. But when he has thus captured their attention, he suddenly switches (in 2:6) to the doom of Israel herself.

(*c*) Chapters 2–6: As a poor man, he is particularly outraged by the unfair distribution and use of Israel's wealth. We would call him today a prophet of social justice. He rages that the rich landlords of Israel "trample the head of the poor into the dust of the earth"; they "turn aside the needy in the gate". But his ideals are not merely philanthropic; he is Yahweh's mouthpiece, and he thunders that for the dissolute rich of Israel there is no escape from the anger of Yahweh. "... as if a man fled from a lion, and a bear met him; or went into a house and leaned with his hand against the wall, and a serpent bit him" (5:19).

(*d*) Chapter 9:   But even in punishing Israel, Yahweh "will
not utterly destroy the house of Jacob".
Yahweh still loves, and will ultimately save,
his people. At least some of this chapter is a
later addition to the preaching of Amos.

Most people who read the Book of Amos leisurely a couple of
times develop a great affection for this simple, honest man, who
had no formal education and no fine words, but who loved
Yahweh and all Yahweh's children, and was not afraid to face
the contempt and hatred of the aristocracy in pleading for the
rights of Yahweh's poor.

The Prophets' Achievement

What, then, did the prophets give to Israel and to Judah—
and what did they transmit to us? First, they looked out over
human history with the eye of faith. They saw, underneath the
ups and downs of daily life, the finger of God tracing a pattern
of events that would finally lead men back to him. They kept alive
the hope that great things lay in store for men. Even in the darkest
hours, they pointed to a messianic dawn. They were men who
received no recognition, no human gratitude, no recompense.
They walked through a dark tunnel of hostility, but continued
steadfastly to promise a golden era at the end of it, an era that not
one of them lived to see.

Secondly, they saw all human life as a continuous tension
between Yahweh's generous love and man's ingratitude and indifference. They insisted on the closeness of Yahweh to even the
least of his children, the closeness of a personal God who loves as
man could never love. Human reason alone could tell men something about God, but in the Old Testament it was only the
prophets who revealed him correctly—as a God who loves, who
cherishes, who chastises reluctantly, and who finally will die for
his own. And that is why a slow and thoughtful reading of the
prophetical books is one of our finest aids to prayer.

CHAPTER 9

The Formation of the Old Testament

AT this point, we may profitably pause to ask a rather fundamental question: Who wrote the Old Testament? In attempting
to answer this question, we shall have an opportunity of taking a
brief look at the whole Old Testament—its books, its formation,
its authors. To so many, the Old Testament is a rather mysterious
area, filled with formidable names like Ecclesiastes, Obadiah and
Habakkuk. We must admit that the Old Testament is rather awe-
some in size; it contains about 900,000 words and almost 900
chapters. Our chief aim in this chapter is to cut a rough path
through this forest of unfamiliar books with strange-sounding
names, and provide a general picture of the Old Testament, what
it contains, and how it came to take its present shape. We can
begin with a few broad general principles.

1. *The Old Testament is not a book; it is a collection of books.*
Even the word "Bible" originated as a plural form; it comes from
the Greek "ta biblia", meaning: "the books". And we still speak of
the Bible as "the scriptures", which means the writings. The Old
Testament found in our Bibles contains forty-six books. These
books fall into three categories or types of writing: historical,
didactic and prophetic. These are general and rather loose divisions,
but they do give a rough indication of what the books contain.

(*a*) The *historical books* are those that concern people and events
in the history of Israel—from the remote beginnings of mankind
to about 130 years before the coming of Christ. Therefore we
count among the historical books everything in the Old Testament
from Genesis to Esther, as well as the two final books, 1 and 2
Maccabees. This makes a total of twenty-one books.

9

(*b*) The *didactic books* are those whose aim is to give moral instruction and advice rather than historical information. This moral instruction Israel handed down normally in poetry, and so these didactic books are mostly in poetic form. There are seven of them: Job, Psalms, Proverbs, Ecclesiastes, Song of Solomon (also called Canticle of Canticles), Wisdom and Ecclesiasticus.

(*c*) The *prophetic books* are those we have been talking about in the last chapter. They are so called because they contain the sermons, and sometimes the life-story, of the significant prophets from the eighth to the fourth century B.C.—the great prophetic age in Israelite history. They include the four great (or major) prophets—Isaiah, Jeremiah, Ezekiel and Daniel, and the twelve lesser (or minor) prophets, thus giving a total of sixteen books, all found together in our Bibles immediately before 1 Maccabees. To these must be added two short books, Lamentations and Baruch, which are normally placed immediately after Jeremiah, because Lamentations is the work of a disciple of Jeremiah, and Baruch was the name of Jeremiah's scribe (*Jer.* 36).

Thus, the Old Testament is not one book—it is a library, a collection of books. And these books are not the work of one man; they are the work of many men, from different areas and different centuries. The Old Testament is the literature of a people—it is the writing down, over a long period, of the memories of a nation. Just as an individual recalls his life and writes down its significant events, so Israel remembered her past and wrote it down. The Old Testament, then, is a collection of books that forms Israel's national library. It is really the autobiography of the Chosen People.

2. *The Old Testament books are very different in format and presentation from the books we are accustomed to.* Modern publishers present us with a book that carries a title, the name of the author, often an outline of his life, and the date of writing. The book generally comes armed with a preface and a table of contents, and is divided into chapters for the readers' convenience.

The compilers and authors of the Old Testament have not been so considerate. Most of the titles of the books were added long after the books appeared, and some of them are misleading. Only one book has a preface—2 Maccabees; and the author puts it at the end of the second chapter.

Again, the Hebrew authors never divided their writing into chapters. They wrote straight through in a continuous manuscript, with no divisions into paragraph, section or chapter. The division of the Old Testament into chapters is the work of an Englishman, Cardinal Stephen Langton, Archbishop of Canterbury, one of the greatest of English scholars, who died in 1228.

But the great difference between an Old Testament book and a modern book is that almost no Old Testament book is the sole work of one man. Most of the books have undergone a process of writing, re-writing, editing, and being added to—so that often it is not possible to speak of the *author* of a particular book. Instead, we must speak of its *authors*, or its *editors*. This procedure of adding to an existing work sometimes went on over several centuries, so that a single Old Testament book may be the result of the collective effort of several men over a period of hundreds of years. As an example of this process, it may be worth looking at the literary history of one of the finest of the Old Testament books, the prophecy of Isaiah.

Isaiah lived and preached in the southern kingdom of Judah in the eighth century B.C. He was a married man, with two sons, and held a high position in the royal palace as adviser to King Ahaz and his successor, King Hezekiah. He seems to have been a well-educated, cultured man; experts in the Hebrew language assure us that he had an exquisite command of the language and a splendid literary style. Even in translation, his poetry is some of the finest in the Old Testament. As a religious man, he is dominated by a tremendous realization of the holiness of God, whom he calls "the Holy One of Israel" (1:4), and is filled with dismay at the laxity and sinfulness of his contemporaries. In 1:23 he writes of them:

> Your princes are rebels
> and companions of thieves.
> Every one loves a bribe
> and runs after gifts.
> They do not defend the fatherless,
> and the widow's cause does not come to them.

For over forty years Isaiah preached, pleaded and warned that the punishment of Yahweh would fall on this nation that had abandoned his covenant and ignored his love. Isaiah foretold the fall of the northern kingdom—and lived to see it happen. He foretold a similar fate for his own Judah and the holy city Jerusalem, but died (Jewish tradition says he was killed) about one hundred years before it happened.

This is the preaching and the message of Isaiah, and this is what is recorded in the book of Isaiah. But not in all of it. This book is a long one of sixty-six chapters, and it is clear that not all these chapters could have come from the eighth century B.C. We can reconstruct approximately how this book came to be compiled.

Chapters 1–35 belong to Isaiah himself and to the eighth century. They contain the preaching and prophecy we have spoken about. Now, at that time, when writing was the luxury of the few, the only way to ensure the preservation of a piece of writing was to hand it on to a group of followers or disciples, who would faithfully copy it and hand it on in turn to their disciples. Isaiah himself, in chapter 8, gives us a picture of how he provided for the transmission of his message. His contemporaries had ignored his preaching, but some future generation would listen to it and learn from it. Therefore, he makes his decision: "Bind up the testimony, seal the teaching among my disciples. I will wait for the Lord, who is hiding his face from the house of Jacob, and I will hope in him" (vv. 16–17).

Isaiah, then, deposited his sermons within the circle of his devoted followers, who treasured them as their master's voice, copied them, revised them in the light of later happenings, and added to them sentiments and sermonettes that breathed the spirit of their dead master.

Thus we find a second section of the present book, chapters 40–55, a section which was written in the sixth century during the Babylonian captivity. These chapters differ in almost every possible way from the first section, and they are referred to as the Book of Second Isaiah, or Deutero-Isaiah. We have no idea who the author was, beyond the fact that he was a follower of Isaiah—

and he was perhaps the supreme poet of the Bible, looking deeper than any other into the golden future of the messianic age. He wrote in Babylon during the exile, because he speaks of the destruction of Jerusalem as a past event, and looks to the end of the captivity and the rebuilding of the holy city. Here there are no threats of approaching punishment, as we find in chapters 1-35, but rather a promise of consolation for the tired and faint-hearted exiles languishing by the alien Euphrates.

The original preaching of Isaiah has now grown considerably. But the development does not stop here. The final chapters of our present book, chapters 56-66, have a new tone, orientation and scenario. The author of these chapters is one who has returned from Babylon, and struggles for the rebuilding of the temple and the restoration of Jewish ritual and worship. Perhaps it is the same author now returned from Babylon; or, which is more likely, a later member of the Isaian prophetic community who, in the fifth century, continued to transmit, in new words, the message and the mood of the Isaiah of the eighth century.

Our Book of Isaiah, then, is really an anthology, and includes, not only the original preaching of Isaiah, but an accumulation of prophecies which, in the opinion of his later but authentic followers, were in keeping with his teaching. You can verify for yourselves that the book shows signs of much editing—it has three distinct introductions: 1:1, 2:1, and chapter 6 (which is the real beginning).

3. A third principle to guide us in understanding the structure of the Old Testament is that, in many cases, *the written book is merely the final stage in a long process of oral tradition*. In the orient of 1000 B.C. writing was a slow, painful, costly, and consequently rare exercise. Therefore the story of God's dealings with men was handed down from generation to generation by word of mouth. With our multiplicity of books and our reliance on the written word, we find it difficult to visualize the important part that memory played among ancient peoples. But, even today, the tenacious memory of oriental people is phenomenal by our slim standards. Much more so, then, in nomadic times, when writing was the monopoly of a few, and clay tablets were too

fragile and cumbersome to survive in a wandering existence. In the era of the Patriarchs and the Judges, from 1800 to 1000 B.C., the normal method of transmitting ideas was by memory, not by writing. Besides, there was something in the Jewish mentality that always, even in New Testament times, preferred the living spoken word to a lifeless document. Therefore, much of Old Testament writing began as a spoken story or poem, a camp-fire saga of God and men that Israelites repeated with reverence. As an example of oral traditions finding their way into written form we may glance at the Pentateuch.

Naturally, we have no first-hand information about how the Pentateuch grew into its present form, and so what scholars say about the process is conjecture. But it is conjecture based on a long and expert examination of the text of the Pentateuch; it is not a sustained flight of imagination.

The story that the Pentateuch tells—the story of the Patriarchs, the exodus and the desert period—began as a list of incidents re-cited by Hebrew story-tellers, who must have been somewhat similar to the old pre-Christian Celtic bards. In Ireland of the fourth and fifth centuries A.D. the Historic Poet or Chronicler occupied an honourable position in the social order. His function was to recount genealogies of the great families, to recite lays of battle, to tell and retell stories in rhyme of voyages, sieges and other important historical events. Sixteen centuries earlier, a roughly similar class of men enjoyed a roughly similar function in Israel. They related the important incidents in Israel's past. These incidents were put in narrative form, to make them interes-ting, and in a repetitive form, to make them easier to remember accurately. Traces of these little memory devices can be seen in our text, in Genesis 2 for instance, which is part of one of the old oral traditions. There, verse 5 says: "when no plant of the field was yet in the earth and no herb of the field had yet sprung up— for the Lord God had not caused it to rain upon the earth, and there was no man to till the ground"; verses 8–15 show the Lord supplying these wants—and in the same order: plant, tree, water, man. A similar example is found in chapter 3, where the dramatis personae appear in this order: serpent, woman,

man—and are sentenced by God in the same order, in verses 14-19.

These simple stories the Hebrews brought with them into Palestine, and they continued to repeat them in a standardized form during the period of the Judges and the early kings. Then, after the death of Solomon, the kingdom split in two, and we have seen how the northern kingdom of Israel and the southern kingdom of Judah continued side-by-side for roughly 200 years. The inhabitants of these kingdoms drifted farther apart, and, as always happens in such cases, there was a growing divergence in language, in idiom, in accent. As part of this natural process, the oral rendering of the salvation story now breaks up into two distinct traditions, one being current in the northern kingdom, the other in the southern. Both relate the same incidents, but with increasing differences in detail. It is these differences that make the literary analysis of the Pentateuch such a fascinating, but also such a tantalizing, exercise.

We now call the northern tradition the "E tradition" and the southern one the "J tradition", the letters being the initials of the Hebrew words they use for God—the northern one calling him "Elohim" and the southern one "Yahweh" (often spelled "Jahweh").

J is written in a very simple colourful style, with great use of imagination. It speaks of God in very human terms. This is the source of Genesis 2 and 3, and there we find God shaping clay like a potter, breathing on it to form man, God planting trees and walking in the afternoon air. Similarly (*Gen.* 18), God eats with Abraham in his tent, and in chapter 32 he wrestles with Jacob on the banks of the river Jabbok. And J includes all the incidents that have the south of Palestine for their scene, for example, J alone tells us of Abraham down south in Hebron.

E, the northern version of the same events, comes on the scene at Genesis 15. It is more fragmentary and more abrupt than J— but also more theological. It does not view God in the childlike manner of its southern parallel; according to E, God is a lofty and dignified figure, who has contact with men chiefly through dreams and visions. For example, Jacob's ladder (*Gen.* 28), Joseph's dreams (*Gen.* 37), Pharaoh's vision (*Gen.* 41)—all belong to this northern stream. And this is the one that mentions the exploits of the Patriarchs in the northern part of Palestine, such as at Bethel.

Now, when the northern kingdom fell in 722 B.C. some refugees from Samaria fled south to Jerusalem, bringing with them their version of the early stages in the salvation story. Thus, it was now possible to unite the two traditions into one single narrative and set them down in fixed written form. It is most interesting to see how the editors (as we may call them) went about this, and a good example of their method is Genesis 37. There you can see how two versions of the same story have been combined—sometimes very happily, sometimes awkwardly. The story is the simple one of Joseph, Jacob's favourite son, the jealousy of his brothers, and their success in getting rid of him by selling him into slavery. If you read it carefully, you will be able to pick out the two distinct versions, each complete in itself, each recounting the full story, but with variations in detail. For example, Joseph's brothers dislike him because Jacob gave him "a long robe with sleeves"—and also because Joseph told them of his dreams. Jacob sends Joseph to the sheep pastures—twice; Reuben saves Joseph from death—twice; and Judah steps in to save him yet again. He is sold as a slave, according to one version to Midianites, according to the other to Ismaelites.

If we today were confronted with two accounts of the same event, we would try to sift out the true details. But what the editors of Genesis did seems surprising to our western eyes. They retained both accounts, with their variations, and welded them roughly into a single story. This editorial method accounts for many of the little discrepancies that tend to annoy us in reading the early sections of the Old Testament.

And the story of the formation of the Pentateuch does not end here. Two more traditions were later joined to the existing union of J and E before the Pentateuch took its present form. The final editing was done after the Babylonian exile, about 500 B.C., by priests of Jerusalem. This activity of codifying Israel's early history formed part of the great rebuilding of city, temple and faith that followed the return from the exile. Our Pentateuch, then, is an ancient and venerable collection of books, whose origins are to be found in the preaching and teaching of Moses, and whose composition was a slow process spanning the centuries from Moses to Nehemiah—a period of over 700 years.

An important question raises its head here. The New Testament calls the Pentateuch "the law of Moses"; the Old Testament calls it "the law of Moses" and "the book of Moses". On this basis, the Church has always accepted the Mosaic authorship of the Pentateuch. But, in the light of the process we have described, what is the meaning of this phrase "Mosaic authorship"? It is neither prudent nor necessary to imagine that Moses wrote every word of the Pentateuch, including Deuteronomy 34, which describes his death! Nor need we picture Moses at the end of the day in the Sinai Peninsula, when the litigants had been pacified and the manna rationed, retiring into his tent, licking a stub of pencil and laboriously writing down the diary of that day's proceedings. It is probable that Moses wrote some kind of résumé of events up to his time, but it makes little difference whether he passed on the information by word of mouth or in writing. The important fact is that the historical function of Moses was to transmit the sacred history and the sacred laws that would rule Israel's life and faith. The nucleus of law and history from which the Pentateuch grew stemmed from Moses. It began as a body of facts and rules transmitted by Moses, and grew ultimately into the national and religious epic of young Israel as we have it. And that is why it is rightly called "the book of Moses".

Now, we seem to have wandered about a little, but we have been trying to present three general principles that help us to understand the composition of the Old Testament. They are important enough to bear repeating.

1. The Old Testament is not a single book but a library, the product of many men and many centuries.

2. Even individual books are often the work of several people, from the original author through his followers to a final editor.

3. Many books have a long history and find their origin in the obscurity of an oral transmission from one generation to the next.

The conclusion that emerges from all this is that often we cannot attach an Old Testament book to any particular man as author. And so the important question to ask is not: *who* wrote the book? but: *when* was it written? Because the date of a book's composition will enable us to put it in historical perspective. We can then read and understand the book against the background of the religious and political conditions out of which it came. So we shall conclude by giving a summary sketch of the growth of the Old Testament library through the centuries.

Chronological Outline

Leaving aside the question of oral tradition, we can put down the reign of Solomon, i.e. *the tenth century*, as the beginning of biblical literature. In that peaceful and prosperous period, a remarkably gifted writer produced the family history of King David, which we find in 2 Samuel 9 — 1 Kings 2. It is one of the finest pieces of prose in the Old Testament—clear, concise, dramatic. This, in the opinion of present-day scholars, was the first section of our Old Testament to be put in writing. We shall say nothing here about the Psalms; we shall speak of them later.

After the division of the kingdom, the first of the writing prophets appear. In *the eighth century* four prophetical books were composed: Amos, Hosea, Micah and Isaiah (chapters 1–35); and after the fall of the northern kingdom in 722 B.C. three more minor prophets wrote.

But the great century of literary activity is *the sixth century*. During this turbulent period most of the Old Testament appeared in writing. Some of it appeared before the Babylonian exile, such as Jeremiah, as well as the final edition of the historical books—Joshua, Judges, the Books of Samuel and Kings. The last tragic years before the fall of Jerusalem are summarized in the turmoil and the urgency of Jeremiah's life and preaching. But his words went unheeded, and the kingdom of Judah went to its doom. In 586 B.C. the Babylonian king captured and sacked Jerusalem, and deported most of its inhabitants to Babylon. A few were left behind, and among them some of the disciples of Jeremiah. These came often to the ruined walls of the temple to recall their hero-prophet's warnings and to weep over their fulfilment. Some of the dirges that they chanted were collected into the little book called Lamentations, and if you have never read it you are missing some of the finest pre-Christian poetry. They were not composed by Jeremiah, but by his followers, in the midst of the desolation that had been proud Jerusalem.

At the same time, prophetic activity was necessary in Babylon to buoy up the crushed spirits of the exiled Israelites. The prophet Ezekiel and the author of Deutero-Isaiah filled this need by fore-telling the return to Jerusalem and the ultimate coming and triumph of a Messiah.

In 537, after the Edict of Cyrus, groups of exiles began making the long trek back to Palestine, and the *following two centuries* see a flurry of literary activity. We have said that the final editing of the Pentateuch belongs to this period—and it came about in this way. Towards the end of the seventh century a "book of the law of Moses", as 2 Kings calls it, was found by the high priest hidden in the temple. This was enlarged and promulgated just before the exile—and is our book of Deuteronomy. This is known, from its initial letter, as the "D tradition" in the Penta-teuch, and was added to the existing J-E combination. Then, during the exile, far removed from temple and law, the exiled priests of the temple composed a new summary of the salvation story; this is now known as the "P tradition" (for "Priestly"). After the return from exile, the temple priests fitted the J-E-D narrative into the framework of the P tradition, and that is why the Pentateuch opens with the P tradition in Genesis 1. You can see immediately that this is more modern and more sophisticated than the other older traditions. For example, when you contrast chapter 1 with chapter 2 you see that the God of Genesis 1 (P) is not one who works with mud or plants trees. Majestically he says: "Let there be light"—and there was light. Besides, Genesis 1 is what we can, alas, call a typical piece of priestly writing—dull, monotonous, full of repetitions. Thus, the Pentateuch is com-posed of four traditions, J-E-D-P.

To this time too belongs the final section of Isaiah (chapters

56–66); and so also do the last of the prophets, Joel and Obadiah, as well as the remainder of the historical books and the final anthology of the Psalms. And in this period we have the appearance of a new type of Old Testament writing—what we call the Wisdom literature, that is, books like Proverbs and Ecclesiastes. These books are collections of proverbs, items of good advice, quotable quotes, etc.—and are hardly the work of any one author.

The final short but bloody struggle against foreign domination and pagan religion is described in the two books of Maccabees, which bring our Old Testament to a close. They were written in the *second century* B.C., immediately after the events they chronicle. They tell the story of the revolt of a family, the sons of Mattathias, against the religious persecution of Antiochus. Though we might be inclined to think so, they are not Volumes 1 and 2 of the same book. They were written at different times, and 2 Maccabees was written about twenty years before 1 Maccabees! And they are so different in style that they are almost certainly written by different men, both equally unknown by name.

During the Maccabean rising the last of the four major prophets, the Book of Daniel, was written. To sustain the embattled Jews in their struggle for freedom of faith and fatherland, an unknown author wrote the story of a good Jew called Daniel, who also suffered for his faith at the hands of a foreign tyrant, but who finally triumphed because God was with him. The moral for the Maccabean Jews was clear.

Finally, Wisdom, the last book of the Old Testament to be written, was also the work of an unknown author. It was written, not in Jerusalem but in Alexandria in Egypt, by one of the Jews of the Diaspora, which means one of those who had wandered out to the great cities all around the Mediterranean coast. The Book of Wisdom was written, as far as we can judge, less than a hundred years before the birth of Christ, during *the first century* B.C. It is a cheerful, optimistic book, and displays a happy marriage between ancient Israelite traditions and the speculative thought of contemporary Greece. In this sense, it forms an ideal and natural bridge between the two Testaments. When St John comes to write his Gospel he will develop many themes already expressed in germ by this unknown Alexandrian Jew, who surely never suspected that his was the honour of being the last literary herald of the Messiah.

Even if this list of names and dates has been confusing, at least one thing must be clear by now, and this is that the Old Testament is the result of a long and collective process. It is a collection of books, whose source of unity is this—that their central character is God, and their common theme is his goodness to ungrateful men. These books have been composed, compiled and collected by the normal slow and stumbling human process of thought and its expression in words. But—and this is what makes the Bible different from every other set of human words—this human process was presided over by the guiding Providence of God in such a way that the finished product is not only the words of men but also the word of God. And that is why we began our voyage through the Old Testament by talking about biblical inspiration.

CHAPTER 10

By the Waters of Babylon

Reading : 2 Kings, chapters 24–5
2 Chronicles, chapter 36
Jeremiah, chapters 21–40
Lamentations, chapters 1–4
Ezekiel, chapters 2–3; 35–7
Isaiah, chapters 40–55
Ezra, chapters 1–10
Nehemiah, chapters 1–6; 12–13

In talking about the kings of Israel and Judah we traced the Old
Testament story up to the death of King Josiah at the battle of
Megiddo in 609 B.C. Now, to set the exile episode in its proper
perspective, we shall continue the history of the kingdom of
Judah up to its final collapse in the summer of 586, that is, the
last twenty-three years of the kingdom. Therefore, the period we
shall be dealing with in this chapter falls into three divisions:

1. Up to the collapse of Jerusalem; for this section the chief
   witness is Jeremiah.
2. The Babylonian captivity; the witnesses here are Ezekiel
   and Deutero-Isaiah.
3. The return from the exile; the chief witnesses are Nehemiah
   and Ezra.

1. Up to the collapse of Jerusalem: 609–586 B.C.

Josiah had been a good king, true to Yahweh and to Judah, and
his reign saw the last period of sincere religion centred around
the temple of Solomon. His death was a sore blow to faith and

fatherland; it brought an abrupt end to the religious revival that was beginning to reap fruit. Tiny Judah's chances of survival were slim in any case, but over the next twenty years a combination of religious indifference and political imprudence hastened the inevitable end.

Josiah's Successors

All this time, great events were taking place away to the east in the Euphrates valley. In 605 Nebuchadnezzar became king of Babylon, and in the same year Babylon became master of all the Assyrian empire. However, Babylon was nearly 1,000 miles from Jerusalem, and probably Judah would have been left in peace if her king had acted intelligently. But King Jehoiakim demonstrated neither religious nor worldly wisdom. He decided to revolt against Nebuchadnezzar, and he persecuted the prophet Jeremiah for daring to protest against this folly. This revolt against the might of the Babylonian empire set in motion the chain of events that culminated in the Babylonian captivity.

In 597 Nebuchadnezzar laid seige to Jerusalem for the first time. During the seige death saved King Jehoiakim from the ignominy of defeat, and his son Jehoiachin succeeded to the throne. His reign lasted only three months, because, when Nebuchadnezzar captured the city, Jehoiachin, his mother, his political advisers and the important citizens of Jerusalem, were carried off to Babylon as prisoners. In this first group of deportees from Jerusalem was a young temple priest called Ezekiel, whom we shall meet again as the first prophet of the exile. Nebuchadnezzar did not destroy the city or despoil the little kingdom; instead he appointed a new king, Zedekiah, and withdrew. This is the story told in 2 Kings 24.

Jeremiah and the last days of Jerusalem

Zedekiah reigned from the first to the second seige of Jerusalem, surely the most disheartening period in the history of the holy city—the eleven years from 597 to 586 B.C. He was the last king of Judah, and he did nothing to reverse the downward trend of the unhappy kingdom. He was not a wicked man, but he was a weak one, an incompetent ruler, unhappily surrounded by obtuse and fanatical advisers. These continued to counsel revolt, and branded as traitor anyone who suggested prudence and patience. Israel's religious heritage, a great trust in Yahweh, her God, had given way to political wishful thinking; and Zedekiah and his advisers preferred to trust in Egyptian aid rather than in divine protection. For nearly ten years the prophet Jeremiah succeeded in keeping Zedekiah from supporting Egypt against Nebuchadnezzar. But in 588 a new Pharaoh came to power in Egypt; Zedekiah bowed to popular pressure and entered a coalition with Egypt to rebel against Babylon. This was Judah's death warrant.

Nebuchadnezzar marched south towards Jerusalem. Thanks to the data supplied by the biblical text, and to the discovery of several Babylonian chronicles, we can date this campaign of Nebuchadnezzar accurately. His powerful army encircled the walls of Jerusalem on 4 January 587, and the famous siege began. Heroically, the city held out for eighteen months, months of increasing famine, distress and helplessness. No piece of writing conveys the atmosphere of that tense period so perfectly as Jeremiah 38, a chapter that gives us a clear picture of the prophet —and of the king. Jeremiah, anxious that his compatriots and his beloved Jerusalem be spared, continues to advise King Zedekiah to surrender quietly to Nebuchadnezzar. He hopes for a repetition of 597, when the city and most of its inhabitants were spared.

> . . . and Pashhur the son of Malchiah heard the words that Jeremiah was saying to all the people, "Thus says the Lord, he who stays in this city shall die by the sword, by famine, and by pestilence; but he who goes out to the Chaldeans shall live; he shall have his life as a prize of war, and live. Thus says the Lord, This city shall surely be given into the hand of the army of the king of Babylon and be taken." Then the princes said to the king, "Let this man be put to death, for he is weakening the hands of the soldiers who are left in this city, and the hands of all the people,

by speaking such words to them. For this man is not seeking the welfare of this people, but their harm." King Zedekiah said, "Behold, he is in your hands; for the king can do nothing against you." So they took Jeremiah and cast him into the cistern of Malchiah, the king's son, which was in the court of the guard, letting Jeremiah down by ropes. And there was no water in the cistern, but only mire, and Jeremiah sank in the mire. (vv. 1–6).

The following verses describe how the king allows Jeremiah to be rescued from the cistern, and then arranges a secret meeting with him. It is a strange and pathetic meeting.

King Zedekiah sent for Jeremiah the prophet and received him at the third entrance of the temple of the Lord. The king said to Jeremiah, "I will ask you a question; hide nothing from me." Jeremiah said to Zedekiah, "If I tell you, will you not be sure to put me to death? And if I give you counsel, you will not listen to me." Then King Zedekiah swore secretly to Jeremiah, "As the Lord lives, who made our souls, I will not put you to death or deliver you into the hand of these men who seek your life" (vv. 14–16).

This is an extraordinary scene. The weakling king knows in his heart that Jeremiah does indeed relay the words of Yahweh, but he is too cowardly to follow the prophet's advice. The circumstances of the meeting are pitiful: the king creeping stealthily from his palace, probably at night, like a criminal, in fear of being seen by his advisers; the whispered conversation in the shadows of the temple gateway; Jeremiah, mud-covered and in rags, having been flogged and starved, yet resolute and invested with divine authority. Externally he is a prisoner, but interiorly he is free, with the freedom that only truth can give; the young king, with all the external trappings of authority, is inwardly the prisoner of his own cowardice. He is a reed shaken by the wind; Jeremiah is the "iron pillar and bronze walls" that God had promised him he would be (1:18), fortified and purified by a life of suffering in the cause of Yahweh. Zedekiah asks again: what will be the outcome of the seige? Jeremiah repeats what he has told him many times: "Thus says the Lord, the God of hosts, the God of Israel, If you will surrender to the princes of the king of Babylon, then your life shall be spared, and this city shall not be burned with fire, and you and your house shall live. But if you do not surrender to the princes of the king of Babylon, then this city shall be given into the hand of the Chaldeans, and they shall burn it with fire, and you shall not escape from their hand" (vv. 17–18).

All in vain. As he turns to go, the king has only one request to make: "Let no one know of these words and you shall not die" (v. 24). Jeremiah seems to pity the weak and tragic king, shields him from his princes, and returns patiently to prison. It is ironic that Jeremiah will be released from prison by Nebuchadnezzar, the conqueror of Jerusalem.

The Babylonian army finally broke through the walls of the city on 19 July 586. Pitiful to the end, Zedekiah abandoned his people and fled through a breach in the walls. He was captured near the river Jordan and dragged ignominiously before Nebuchadnezzar. Jeremiah records his cruel fate in 39:6–7: "The king of Babylon slew the sons of Zedekiah at Riblah before his eyes; and the king of Babylon slew all the nobles of Judah. He put out the eyes of Zedekiah, and bound him in fetters to take him to Babylon."

Nebuchadnezzar spent a month rounding up the greater part of the population of Jerusalem and the surrounding villages and forming them into long lines to march to Babylon. Everything of value was taken from the temple and the palaces. The city walls were torn down, and, on 19 August 586, the departing army set fire to the city and the temple. Judah was at an end. The Babylonian captivity had begun. It is on this sad note that the Books of Kings end, as you see by glancing through 2 Kings 25.

The holy city, the royal capital since 1000 B.C., is a mass of blackened ruins. Those who are left behind wander through this ghost land and remember the proud city of David and the gleaming temple of Solomon. Some of their sad reflections have been preserved for us in the little book called Lamentations, associated in our minds with the haunting melodies of Tenebrae in Holy Week.

> The elders of the daughter of Zion
> sit on the ground in silence;
> they have cast dust on their heads
> and put on sackcloth;
> the maidens of Jerusalem
> have bowed their heads to the gorund.
>
> What can I say for you, to what compare you,
> O daughter of Jerusalem?
> What can I liken to you, that I may comfort you,
> O virgin daughter of Zion?
> For vast as the sea is your ruin;
> who can restore you?
>
> All who pass along the way
> clap their hands at you;
> they hiss and wag their heads
> at the daughter of Jerusalem;
> "Is this the city which was called
> the perfection of beauty,
> the joy of all the earth?" (*Lament.* 2:10; 13; 15).

2. *In Exile: 586–537* B.C.

From the carvings on Assyrian and Babylonian monuments we get a picture of what the deportation to Babylon was like. We can give no reliable number for those deported; 30,000 is a figure generally accepted. They were assembled at Ramah, five miles north of Jerusalem, in a kind of concentration camp, and there they were arranged in long columns, bound to one another by ropes, and marched off to Babylon. From the Jordan valley to the Euphrates valley is a distance of over 700 miles, and the journey must have taken about two months. During this cruel forced-march in the autumn of 586, many must have died on the way; this was the normal occurrence in slave marches of the time. No section of the Bible gives us any information about this journey.

Nor does the Bible tell us much about the conditions under which the exiles lived in Babylon from 586 to after 537. From

Ezekiel we can conclude that many of them lived beside the river Chebar, near the city of Nippur. However enslaved their first years in exile may have been, they soon came to enjoy a considerable measure of freedom. They built houses and had little farms, and gradually formed themselves into villages, one of which, Ezekiel tells us, they called Tel-Aviv. Some of them began to engage in commerce, and with the financial wizardry and tenacious industry still characteristic of their descendants, they grew wealthy and influential.

They saw Babylon at the peak of its prosperity. The Babylonian empire was short-lived—only about seventy years—but they were years of lavish splendour. The glory of the city of Babylon is still dimly visible in the ruins uncovered by successive excavations— the magnificent Ishtar Gate, the ziggurat that towered over the city, the enamelled brickwork with intricate designs and figures, the famous "hanging gardens" high on the terraces and flat roofs. In this affluent society it was probably easy to get rich quickly, and recent archeological discoveries prove that several of the exiles did prosper. American excavations at Nippur brought to light hundreds of clay tablets that turned out to be the business files of a Jewish banking firm—Murashu and Sons. These documents show that this Jewish family did business—chiefly in money-changing—not only with fellow-Jews, but with Babylonians and anyone who traded in that international market area.

The Old Testament, not being a textbook of secular history, tells us little about the exiles' material circumstances. But, since it is a theology of history, it concentrates on their spiritual and moral conditions, and the religious ideas that were at work among them.

Ezekiel's Ministry

The obliteration of the Davidic kingdom, and the reduction of the Israelites to slavery in a foreign land, presented them with the greatest single crisis in their history. And it was a specifically religious crisis. Yahweh was their God. The conquering Babylonians jeered that the gods of Babylon were obviously superior to the God of Israel. The fall of Jerusalem was interpreted, not merely as the defeat of a people, but as the defeat of that people's God. The temptation to join with their masters in worshipping the imposing idols of Babylon was a pressing one. It was this crucial problem that confronted the young Ezekiel, when he received the prophetic call by the river Chebar. It is a measure of Ezekiel's greatness, and of his right to be called a major prophet, that he was able to turn the exile from a period of dismal despair into years of reflection, repentance and hope.

First, he set out to convince the exiles that their present abject state was not a defeat of Yahweh, but a punishment from Yahweh. It is not Yahweh who has failed his people, but they who have failed him. They had abandoned the religion of their fathers and the covenant of Sinai, and now Yahweh, God of all nations and of all history, has used their pagan neighbours as an instrument to chastise them. In chapter 20 Ezekiel traces Israel's long history of infidelity to Yahweh—and requires forty-nine verses to give even some samples of it!

In spite of their pitiful record, however, Yahweh has neither abandoned nor forgotten his people. This nation, defeated and humiliated in the eyes of the entire orient, will yet see a glorious resurrection. The former prophets of Israel have not spoken fantasies. Yahweh has not gone down in defeat. Israel as a kingdom was dead, but Yahweh can restore her, even from the grave. Ezekiel relayed to them his splendid vision of the valley of dry bones. At this point it is worth turning at once to chapter 37 and reading the first ten verses of it. What images and memories the very mention of bones must have brought to the exiles' minds! They had seen them on their sad journey from Jerusalem—the bleached skeletons of their brothers who had fallen and died in the long march through the desert.

Ezekiel continues in chapter 37:

> Then he said to me, "Son of man, these bones are the whole house of Israel. Behold, they say, Our bones are dried up, and our hope is lost; we are clean cut off. Therefore prophesy, and say to them, Thus says the Lord God: Be-

hold, I will open your graves, and raise you from your graves,
O my people; and I will bring you home into the land of
Israel!" (vv. 11–12).

Later on in the same chapter he says:

> Thus says the Lord God: Behold, I will take the people of
> Israel from the nations among which they have gone, and
> will gather them from all sides, and bring them to their own
> land; and I will make them one nation in the land, upon the
> mountains of Israel; and one king shall be king over them all;
> and they shall be no longer two nations, and no longer
> divided into two kingdoms. They shall not defile themselves
> any more with their idols and their detestable things, or with
> any of their transgressions; but I will save them from all the
> backslidings in which they have sinned, and will cleanse
> them; and they shall be my people, and I will be their God
> (vv. 21–3).

This ancient formula of Sinai must have fallen like soft music
on their ears.

Ezekiel had been a priest of the Jerusalem temple, and his
thoughts were always there. The last nine chapters of his book
speak exclusively of a new temple, a new and more faithful
gathering of worshippers, and a restored ritual of prayer and
sacrifice. But what shall they do for prayer and sacrifice in the
Euphrates valley—700 miles from the site of the temple of
Yahweh? The custom gradually grew up of coming together,
presumably in the house of one of the exiled priests, to worship
Yahweh. Sacrifice was out of the question, because they associated
sacrifice exclusively with the temple. So they assembled and read
some passages from their early history, which were explained and
amplified by somebody expert in the Mosaic law. Out of these
meetings came the post-exilic institution of the synagogue, where
local Jewish communities gathered to sing hymns and read the
Old Testament. The word "synagogue" means "bringing
together". And synagogue always remained distinct from temple;
in the New Testament we find that every Jewish community had

its local synagogue, but only Jerusalem had a temple of Yahweh.

In these meetings they listened again to the voice of the early prophets, Amos, Hosea, Isaiah—and their thoughts turned back to the story of the Patriarchs and the origins of the salvation drama. From this reflection, and as an aid to it, the exiled priests assembled a new version of Hebrew origins, which became the "P tradition" we have spoken of in connection with the Pentateuch. At these gatherings they sang again, now with sorrow, the ancient temple chants of Yahweh, and to them they added new ones, expressing their homesickness for the temple. One of these, or a song based on it, has been preserved in Psalm 137.

> By the waters of Babylon,
> there we sat down and wept,
> when we remembered Zion.
> On the willows there
> we hung up our lyres.
> For there our captors
> required of us songs,
> and our tormentors, mirth, saying,
> "Sing us one of the songs of Zion!"
> How shall we sing the Lord's song
> in a foreign land?
> If I forget you, O Jerusalem,
> let my right hand wither!
> Let my tongue cleave to the roof of my mouth,
> if I do not remember you,
> if I do not set Jerusalem
> above my highest joy! (vv. 1–6).

Deutero-Isaiah—A Universal Salvation

The desire to sing the songs of Yahweh once more in Yahweh's own house joined hands with Ezekiel's vision of a return to provide an invincible hope of a restoration of Yahweh's people. Gradually they came to understand that they were being chastened and purified by the hand of God—not unto destruction but unto restoration. At this point another prophet came providentially on the scene to put their historical destiny before them in its proper perspective. This unknown prophet is the man we call, for want of a better name, Deutero-Isaiah, and what he preached is now found in poetic form in Isaiah 40–55.

This anonymous prophet of the exile was probably the supreme poet of the Old Testament, and to majestic language he joined a breadth of vision that could have only God for its author. He saw, as no one before him had seen, that Israel had been chosen by God, not merely for her own sake, but that she might be the channel of divine blessings on all men. The deliverance from the exile was close at hand, he told his audience, and this deliverance would ultimately touch all mankind, even the most distant nations. It would be a deliverance both material and spiritual—a new exodus from Babylon and from sinfulness; it would be a deliverance both local and universal—for Judah and for all the world. Therefore Isaiah thunders God's message to the boundaries of the world:

> Turn to me and be saved,
> all the ends of the earth!
> For I am God, and there is no other (45:22).

Yahweh is about to lead Israel out of the darkness, and she will become a light to the nations:

> Fear not, for I am with you;
> I will bring your offspring from the east,
> and from the west I will gather you;
> I will say to the north, Give up,
> and to the south, Do not withhold;
> Let all the nations gather together,
> And let the peoples assemble (43:5–6; 9).

Deutero-Isaiah calls on pagan cities and the distant islands of the Mediterranean to join in a world-wide chorus of praise to Yahweh, the one true God.

> Sing to the Lord a new song,
> his praise from the end of the earth!
> Let the sea roar and all that fills it,
> the coastlands and their inhabitants.
> Let the desert and its cities lift up their voice,
> the villages that Kedar inhabits;
> let the inhabitants of Sela sing for joy,
> let them shout from the top of the mountains.
> Let them give glory to the Lord,
> and declare his praise in the coastlands (42:10–12).

Nowhere else in the Old Testament do we find the true destiny of Israel so clearly expressed; nowhere else is there so broad a vision of humanity; nowhere else so perfect a foretelling of the missionary endeavour of the future Church of Christ.

A Suffering Messiah

The concept of the Messiah also takes a giant stride forward in the prophecy of Deutero-Isaiah. Not alone did Deutero-Isaiah add his voice to Israel's older prophets in foretelling the coming of a deliverer, a redeemer, but more than any of them he pierced into the mystery of God's saving act, and foresaw vaguely how the redemption would be accomplished. He foretold a Messiah who would be glorious and triumphant, but through suffering and humiliation. This was a hard and almost incomprehensible message to oriental people, who knew victory only as military domination, and recognized triumph only in the regalia of monarchs. The prophet himself foresaw only dimly, and even to us, living in the era of fulfilment, his words are still mysterious.

His messianic vision reached its apex in four splendid pieces of poetry that we know as the Servant Songs. You must read them —and several times. They are:

> Isaiah 42:1–4
> 49:1–7
> 50:4–9
> 52:13–53:12

In reading these passages, you will notice that sometimes the "Servant" seems to be simply the Israelite nation, as in 49:3, "You are my servant, Israel." But in other passages the Servant is an individual—a man of royal mien but sorrow-stricken life; this is especially the picture given in the fourth song—"a man of sorrows".

Discussion will always surround the identity of the mysterious figure of the Servant. But a certain transition from nation to individual and back again is built into the text itself, and really represents the lack of detail in the prophet's pre-vision. As always, we understand his message a little better when we recall its historical background.

Deutero-Isaiah, writing during the exile—and in exile—saw Israel as suffering for her past infidelities, but being purified through her suffering. At some point of time, this suffering will end, and Israel will be closer to Yahweh as a result of it. By prophetic illumination, the writer sees Israel as a model of the Messiah to come. However, the Messiah will surpass Israel in many respects. First, he will suffer, not for his own infidelities, but innocently for those of others. Secondly, Israel suffers under protest and by force of historical circumstances—she has no alternative; the Messiah will suffer willingly, offering himself— "he opened not his mouth". Again, his victory will surpass Israel's resurrection from exile and despondency; his victory will be definitive, universal and complete. In the circumstances of Deutero-Isaiah, it is easy enough to see why his thought passed to and fro between the nation of Israel and the person of the Messiah so frequently.

In spite of the limited nature of his prophetic vision, Deutero-Isaiah sketched, more eloquently and more accurately than any other Old Testament writer, a portrait of Christ—humble, suffering, but eternally triumphant.

Cyrus and Freedom

Thus, as the fifty years of exile draw to a close, God's designs for his stubborn and rebellious people take a step nearer their final goal. A new generation has been born in captivity, and they grow up in an atmosphere of repentance and humble conversion of heart. The exiles understand their duty and their destiny better than did the proud inhabitants of Palestine in the days of the kings. They look to a golden future that is not one of political aggrandisement for Israel, but rather a spiritual reunion of all mankind in the worship of Yahweh. It is remarkable, but hardly accidental, that Israel's clearest vision of humanity came to her during the exile. The exile destroyed Israel politically, but it restored Israel spiritually. It sent Israel among the nations, not as a conqueror but as a captive. No longer a material kingdom, the Israelites became a community of believers, a Church in germ. And as their material ambitions shrank, their spiritual horizons widened.

As always, God used the historical circumstances of the time, the rise and fall of nations, to achieve his plans. Just as he had used the young Babylonian empire to punish his people, so now he used the fall of Babylon to liberate them. The collapse of Babylon was sudden and complete. Cyrus, king of the Persians, conquered the kingdom of the Medes in 550 B.C. Now king of both Medes and Persians, he pushed on in search of greater triumphs and larger territory. Eventually he reached Babylon, an empire steadily in decline since the death of Nebuchadnezzar. It took Cyrus only two days to capture the city of Babylon. The date is 539 B.C.

Cyrus displayed none of the harsh ruthlessness of other oriental conquerors. He seems to have been broadminded and tolerant, and, as far as the Judean exiles were concerned, he was liberator rather than conqueror. Soon after his occupation of Babylon he issued the famous Edict of Cyrus allowing the exiles to return home. The Book of Ezra transmits it in these words:

> Thus says Cyrus king of Persia: The Lord, the God of heaven, has given me all the kingdoms of the earth, and he has charged me to build him a house at Jerusalem, which is in Judah. Whoever is among you of all his people, may his God be with him, and let him go up to Jerusalem, which is

in Judah, and rebuild the house of the Lord, the God of Israel—he is the God who is in Jerusalem; and let each survivor, in whatever place he sojourns, be assisted by the men of his place with silver and gold, with goods and with beasts, besides freewill offerings for the house of God which is in Jerusalem (1:2–4).

3. Return and Rebuilding: 537—about 400 B.C.

The Edict of Cyrus was more than a mere permission for the Israelites to return to their homeland. Cyrus actively assisted them; he gave money from the Persian treasury to help in rebuilding the Jerusalem temple, and restored to it the valuable vessels that Nebuchadnezzar had confiscated. He appointed Sheshbazzar as leader of the returning exiles. He was a son of Jehoiachin, and therefore a prince of the line of David. All these developments must have kindled in the hearts of the homeward-bound exiles hopes that a new and glorious kingdom of Israel was at hand. This seemed the fulfilment of the consoling prophecy of Deutero-Isaiah:

> Shake yourself from the dust, arise;
> O captive Jerusalem;
> loose the bonds from your neck,
> O captive daughter of Zion.
>
> Break forth together into singing,
> you waste places of Jerusalem;
> for the Lord has comforted his people,
> he has redeemed Jerusalem (*Is.* 52:2; 9).

According to Ezra 2, over 42,000 people set out on the long trek back to Palestine. Many refused to leave, and they seem to have been the ones who had grown prosperous in exile. But we should not rush to condemn them as apostates. Ezra and Nehemiah tell how those who remained in Babylon sent large sums of money to help in the rebuilding of the city and the temple. In fact, the situation seems somewhat similar to that existing in modern

Israel. Many wealthy American and British Jews have no intention of returning to Israel, living in a kibbutz and driving a tractor in Galilee, but they do contribute to the welfare of the little nation by generous dollar-transfusions.

The returning exiles, then, were a tightly-knit, select group, driven by deep religious fervour. But they were only a section of the kingdom of Judah, and only a tiny minority of the ancient twelve tribes. This is the promised "remnant" of the house of David, a chosen group through which the salvation plan will be unfolded. And so we call them no longer Israelites but *Jews*. The word "Yehudi" means a descendant of the people who formerly occupied Judah. So, from this onward, we shall speak of Jews and Judaism.

Many of them, born in exile, were coming into Palestine for the first time. And they were bringing with them a new language—Aramaic. Up to the exile, Hebrew had been their national language, the language in which they prayed, and the language in which most of the Old Testament was written. In Babylon they came into contact with Aramaic, a language very close to Hebrew which they had little difficulty in learning. The Persian empire used Aramaic as its official language, and so gradually it became the language of daily life in Palestine. This was the situation at the time of Christ; Aramaic was the language he spoke, and we have all picked up some Aramaic words from the New Testament, such as abba, talitha cumi, mammon.

Rebuilding the Ruins

The return to Palestine meant return to a ravaged and poverty-stricken land. Their capital city lay in ruins, much of the surrounding countryside had been taken over by the hostile Samaritans from the north, and a sharp struggle for material survival occupied the first months after the return. The leader of the group during the early stages was Zerubbabel, another descendant of the line of David, and he directed his efforts chiefly to remedying the social ills—finding houses and lands in which to re-settle the exiles. Only when this was done did he turn to the rebuilding of the temple. Although begun in 536, it was not completed and dedicated until 515. There were several reasons for this slow progress: (*a*) the poverty of the Jews; they depended entirely on those in Babylon for financial assistance; (*b*) the opposition of the Samaritans, who resented the return of the Jews as an intrusion on the lands of Judah, which the Samaritans had largely confiscated; (*c*) the disillusionment of many of the returned exiles. They had come back bathed in the glow of rosy messianic prophecies, but their first fervour soon evaporated in the face of harsh daily realities, and the struggle to rebuild the ravaged city. Only the encouragement of the prophet Haggai prodded them to work on: ". . . work, for I am with you, says the Lord of hosts, according to the promise that I made you when you came out of Egypt. My Spirit abides among you; fear not . . . The latter splendour of this house shall be greater than the former, says the Lord of hosts . . ." (*Hag.* 2:4–5; 9).

Next on the scene came Nehemiah, one of the great figures of this period. He set about rebuilding the city walls. As they worked at this, the Samaritans gathered to jeer at them: "'What are these feeble Jews doing? Will they restore things? Will they sacrifice? Will they finish up in a day? Will they revive the stones out of the heaps of rubbish, and burned ones at that?' Tobiah the Ammonite was by him, and he said, 'Yes, what they are building—if a fox goes up on it he will break down their stone wall!'" (*Neh.* 4:2–3).

This was one of the memories that rankled in Jewish minds, and gave rise to the New Testament situation: "Jews have no dealings with Samaritans" (*John* 4:9). However, in spite of the scorn and threats of the Samaritans, Nehemiah and his Jews kept on building, and Nehemiah 12 tells how the new city walls were blessed in a solemn ceremony and procession.

While all this material building was on foot, Ezra, called the father and founder of Judaism, was working towards a spiritual rebuilding of faith. He organized great feasts on which the Mosaic law was read publicly to all the people in Jerusalem. Under his guidance, the Jews solemnly renewed the Mosaic covenant with Yahweh, and their leaders signed a covenant document on behalf of all the people, promising under oath "to walk in God's law which was given by Moses the servant of God" (*Neh*. 10:29).

Thus the Jews are home again in the Promised Land. But under very different circumstances. There is no kingdom and no king. They are ruled officially by a civil governor appointed by Persia. This, then, is Judaism: the children of Abraham no longer a nation but a community of worshippers of Yahweh, clustered around Jerusalem and the second temple. They loved this temple —they had built it, stone by stone, in the teeth of grinding poverty, the scorn of their enemies and the indifference of many fellow-Jews. Around this temple they centred all their religion and all their hopes for the future. And in this post-exilic period they gathered together all their sacred songs to form the hymn-book of the second temple—the Book of Psalms.

CHAPTER 11

Israel at Prayer

So far, we have seen Israel at war and at peace, at sacrifice and at work. Now it is time to listen to Israel at prayer. The religious life of a man can be measured by his prayer, and the same is true of a nation. By studying Israel at prayer we can learn much about the flame of faith that burned, sometimes brightly, sometimes dimly, but was never quite extinguished, in Israel. The Israelites always prayed; they prayed naturally, openly; prayer was for them a normal, uncomplicated act. The historical books of the Old Testament contain many examples of beautiful public prayers offered at great moments in their history, as in 2 Chronicles 6—the prayer at the dedication of Solomon's temple, and in Ezra 9—the public act of contrition of the returned exiles.

However, in the reorganization of temple and faith that took place after the return from Babylon, the Jews assembled their public ceremonial poem-prayers into what we call the Book of Psalms. This official hymnbook of Judaism became a part of the life of every pious Jew, and on these religious songs the thought of the early Christian Church was nourished. Even today, 2,400 years after this anthology of hymns was assembled, it is still the most familiar and most beloved part of the Old Testament to Christians everywhere. We have all heard, read and sung psalms many times; we are accustomed to applying them roughly to our own moods and circumstances. In this chapter we shall attempt to answer two questions: (*a*) How did these psalms take shape originally, and what did they mean to the Old Testament Jews who recited them? (*b*) What value can these ancient prayers have for us—non-Jews of the Western world in the space age?

Hebrew Poetry

The Psalter is a collection of 150 psalms, an anthology of sacred songs. Since they are poems, they have all the literary characteristics of the oriental poetry of their time. Many scholars have studied the psalms simply as pieces of literature. For us, however, the psalms are more than poetry; but we need not, and should not, be blind to their beauty or deaf to their harmony. For us, the psalms are inspired poems, and therefore they bring us into contact with the God who speaks to men in their own language. Thus they have, for all men everywhere, meaning and message beyond any other collection of poetry.

Hebrew poetry is constructed chiefly in terms of rhythm rather than metre. English poetry tends to shape itself according to metre—a definite arrangement of groups of syllables, for instance iambic, having two syllables, with the accent on the second, thus:

"And *leaves* the *world* to *dark*ness *and* to *me*."

In Hebrew poetry there is greater freedom and flexibility, since it is based on rhythm, that is, a regular number of accented syllables, which may have few or many unstressed syllables between them. Naturally, this rhythmic formation based on tonic accents is lost in translation into a European language. But the translators of the Jerusalem Bible decided, however, to attempt to reproduce it in their French translation of the psalms. It was this translation that a French Jesuit, Fr Gelineau, used for his new psalm melodies. Then an English translation was made, supervised by the Grail, to suit Gelineau's music; thus it conveys some of the Hebrew rhythm. For example, the Douay translation of Psalm 41:3 reads: "My soul hath thirsted after the strong living God; when shall I come and appear before the face of God?"

In the English translation for Gelineau's music this is how the same verse sounds:

My *soul* is *thirst*ing for *God*,
the *God* of my *life*;
when can *I* en*ter* and *see*
the *face* of *God*?

This type of translation brings us closer to the rugged rhythm of the Hebrew verse.

However, the dominant characteristic of Hebrew poetry is its *parallelism*, and this is found in different forms all through the psalms. Most verses are in two parts, and parallelism means simply that the two parts run side-by-side in thought content, or express the same idea in different ways. Therefore the real basis for the poetic structure is arrangement of thought rather than arrangement of words. Psalm 2:3–4 provides an example:

> "Let us burst their bonds asunder,
> and cast their cords from us."
> He who sits in the heavens laughs;
> the Lord has them in derision.

Sometimes this parallelism is worked out by contrast rather than by repetition, as here in Psalm 20:7–8:

> Some boast of chariots, and some of horses;
> but we boast of the name of the Lord our God.
> They will collapse and fall;
> but we shall rise and stand upright.

Because the psalms were public hymns, sung chiefly in the temple by the assembled worshippers, they were specially constructed for community singing. Some traces of this are easily seen. (*a*) *Refrain*—the repetition of the same set of words after a fixed number of verses. For example, if you read Psalm 42, you will notice that verses 5 and 11 are similar. And because Psalm 43:5 repeats the same phrase, it is a reasonable conclusion that these two psalms originally formed one psalm of sixteen verses, broken into three sections by the refrain. Presumably, the psalm was sung by a temple choir or chanters, while the whole congregation joined in the refrain. (*b*) *Litany*—Some of the psalms are in litany form, with the congregation replying to every verse. The best example of this is Psalm 136:

> O give thanks to the Lord of lords,
> for his steadfast love endures for ever;
> to him who alone does great wonders,

> for his steadfast love endures for ever;
> to him who by understanding made the heavens,
> for his steadfast love endures for ever (vv. 3–5).

(c) *Alphabetic Psalms*—Some psalms used alphabetic succession of initial letters as an aid to the worshippers' memory, for example Psalms 25, 34, 111, 112, 119. Since there were twenty-two letters in the Hebrew alphabet, the length of the psalm is determined by this; some have eleven verses, others twenty-two, and Psalm 119 (the longest in the Psalter) has one hundred and seventy-six verses (=8×22). This kind of alphabet game is reproduced by Mgr Knox in his translation of the psalms. His version of Psalm 111:1–3 runs like this:

> All my heart goes out to thee, Lord, in thanksgiving,
> before the assembly where the just are gathered.
> Chant we the Lord's wondrous doings,
> decreed to fulfil all his purposes.
> Ever his deeds are high and glorious,
> faithful he abides to all eternity.

Psalms and David

It has always been conventional to refer to the psalms as the "Psalms of David". In the Bible many of them bear that title. The titles of the psalms are an intriguing study. For example, Psalm 4 has the following title: "To the choirmaster: with stringed instruments. A Psalm of David." These are rather obscure statements, but they seem to refer mainly to the musical and liturgical setting of the psalm. But what is the meaning of the final phrase: "A Psalm of David"?

It is now certain that the psalms, as we have them, were not all composed at the same time. Many of them do belong to the period of the kings, and there is no reason to doubt that some of these are of Davidic authorship. Other psalms were composed during the exile, and many more came into being only in the era of the Second Temple. But in assembling the psalms, the priests of the Second Temple did not arrange them in chronological order, and we depend on references in the text and on the atmosphere of individual psalms for hints to their date of composition.

However, the whole collection has always been associated with David, and for this reason: that it is an expansion of a nucleus of ceremonial hymns that have David for their author. The Books of Samuel and Chronicles tell us that David organized ritual and worship around the Ark of the Covenant; you may remember what we said about Jerusalem as a religious centre. 2 Samuel also tells us that David composed sacred songs; in fact, if you compare the two texts, you will see that 2 Samuel 22 writes down Psalm 18 as a "song" of David. We must, then, grant to David an essential role in forming the origins of the religious poetry of Israel. The initial impulse given by him was taken up by later poets, so that our present Book of Psalms, while stemming from David, really embraces several centuries of Israelite poetic activity.

Psalm Categories

To take up the Psalter, begin reading at Psalm 1 and continue doggedly right through to Psalm 150, may not be a very rewarding experience. To take them in the chronological order in which they were written—first the psalms of the kingdom, then those of the exile, and finally those of the Second Temple—would be a better idea. But it is not possible, because the date of composition of several psalms still eludes us. Thus, a far more enriching experience is to read the psalms according to the different categories or families into which they fall. The three great families of psalms, easily distinguished from one another, are: Hymns of Praise; Psalms of Supplication or Lamentation; Songs of Thanksgiving. Psalms of Supplication and of Thanksgiving may be of two kinds; some are personal—an individual petitioning or thanking on his own behalf; others are national—a community plea or community "Te Deum" on behalf of Israel as a unit. Apart from these prominent divisions, there are several psalms that we recognize as Pilgrimage Psalms—ones sung on the way to the temple for the great feasts. Also, there is a group best called Coronation Psalms, or Psalms of Enthronement. They seem to have been chanted in solemn processions in Jerusalem, and they are really hymns of praise to Yahweh as king. They describe the universal dominion of Yahweh over all the earth and its creatures, and they look forward to the continuation of this kingship of Yahweh forever. Psalm 47 is one of these.

> For God is the king of all the earth;
> sing praises with a psalm!
> God reigns over the nations;
> God sits on his holy throne.
> The princes of the peoples gather
> as the people of the God of Abraham (vv. 7–9).

Other Psalms of Enthronement are: Psalms 68; 93; 96; 97.

Close to these in form and sentiment are the Royal Psalms, some of the oldest in the Psalter—coming from the days of the kings. They speak of the reigning king as Yahweh's representative, preserving and leading Yahweh's earthly kingdom; they regard the king as inheriting and transmitting the great promises made to the house of David. But these psalms always look beyond the reigning human king to a greater and enduring king, and so it is in this family of psalms that we find the principal messianic passages in the Psalter. Psalms 2, 20, 21, 45 and 72 are examples of this category.

Anyone who keeps in mind an outline of the characteristic structure and theme of each of these psalm families, and then reads slowly one or two typical psalms from each family, has already gathered much useful knowledge about how the Book of Psalms is composed and what it contains. In the next few pages we shall try to show how such a summary view of the Psalter might be built up.

Hymns of Praise

These are about twenty-five in number, and from their structure and wording they seem to have been associated exclusively with the temple. Their general theme is the goodness of God to Israel. They express joy and enthusiasm in praising him; they run easily to exuberance. They strain language and imagery to shout out how wonderful God is, and how wonderful it is to be a member of his chosen race. They praise him as Creator, and call on all created things to join in his worship. They recall the exodus, his greatest saving act.

Normally this type of psalm falls into three parts:

1. *Introduction*—an invitation to praise God.
2. *Main Theme*—giving the motives for praise—generally God's past goodness to Israel.
3. *Conclusion*—God's past goodness still continues, and is eternal.

A good example of this category is Psalm 29, which is still used in the modern Jewish liturgy as a hymn for the Feast of Weeks, or Pentecost.

1. *Introduction*: (vv. 1–2).

> Ascribe to the Lord, O heavenly beings,
> ascribe to the Lord glory and strength.
> Ascribe to the Lord the glory of his name;
> worship the Lord in holy array.

"Sons of God" would be a more accurate translation of the Hebrew text than "heavenly beings" in verse 1, and most scholars understand the phrase to mean the Israelites gathered in the temple, who are mentioned in verse 9. The reference to "worship the Lord" suggests that this song was composed for a solemn temple sacrifice, and the "holy array" is probably the "Sunday best" of the worshipping Israelites.

2. *Main Theme*: (vv. 3–9). As you read these verses, you will have no difficulty in finding the central theme, because the phrase "the voice of the Lord" is repeated seven times. From the context "the voice of the Lord" means the thunder, or perhaps in general the noise of the great storm that is being described here. Therefore the psalm is praising the God of nature, the God who sends the storm before which men bend in fear. And here is its fittingness as a psalm for the Jewish Pentecost, which was a harvest

thanksgiving festival. The God of nature has blessed their land, their vineyards, their crops; he has held back the storm that would destroy their year's labour. And we can also see the providential fittingness of this psalm as a hymn for the Christian Pentecost, when the Spirit came down on frightened men as the voice of the Lord—"a sound . . . like the rush of a mighty wind" (*Acts* 2).

In reciting this psalm, the Israelites praised God for the storm, which was a manifestation to all the world of the magnificence and sublimity of Yahweh. A storm demonstrates his easy mastery over all created things: the giant cedars of Lebanon crash to the ground; lightning strikes the waterless "wilderness of Kadesh" where their forefathers had sweltered in the desert; the Mediterranean swells to a raging flood—"many waters"—in mute submission to "the voice of the Lord".

3. *Conclusion:* (vv. 10–11).

> The Lord sits enthroned over the flood;
> The Lord sits enthroned as a king for ever.
> May the Lord give strength to his people!
> May the Lord bless his people with peace!

The tempest will pass, but God remains, loving and blessing his own people. Yahweh's power is terrifying, but his faithful friends have nothing to fear. He will "bless his people with peace". "Shalom", meaning peace, has always been, and still is, the Jewish address of greeting. To their minds, peace meant much more than the absence of war; it signified the accumulation of all good things: peaceful possession of their own land, the prosperity that flows from this undisputed tenure, and the peace of mind coming from friendly relations with God and men.

It is worth noticing that the psalm begins with a universal call to give glory to God and ends with a promise of peace from God. As Mgr Patrick Boylan aptly remarks, Psalm 29 begins with: Glory to God in the highest, and ends with: peace on earth to men of goodwill.

All the Hymns of Praise follow approximately the same pattern. Other examples of this type are: Psalms 8, 19, 33, 145, 148.

Songs of Personal Thanksgiving

A group rather similar to the Hymns of Praise is the family of psalms we call Songs of Personal Thanksgiving. But here the motives for praising God are more concrete and particularized—the singer praises God for some specific example of divine goodness recently experienced in his own life.

From references in the text of these Psalms of Personal Thanksgiving it seems clear that they were generally sung on the occasion of an official sacrifice of thanksgiving in the temple. The words are intended to accompany a liturgical action. This ceremonial act of gratitude had three parts: 1. An entry into the temple; 2. A recitation of God's benefits; 3. The offering of a sacrifice.

1. *Entry:* The Israelite who has received the favour from God, who has been delivered from danger, etc., arrives, grateful and rejoicing, at the gates of the temple. There he announces to all his intention of offering a sacrifice of thanks:

> Open to me the gates of righteousness,
> that I may enter through them
> and give thanks to the Lord.
> This is the gate of the Lord;
> the righteous shall enter through it.
> I thank thee that thou hast answered me
> and hast become my salvation (*Ps.* 118:19–21).

2. *Recitation of benefits:* This is the thanksgiving proper. The singer tells everybody in the temple that when he was in danger he called on God and God heard his prayer. He presents himself to the congregation as a living witness to the divine goodness, and often launches into a long sermon in general terms on God's goodness and the reasons for trusting in him:

> Out of my distress I called on the Lord;
> the Lord answered me and set me free.
> With the Lord on my side I do not fear.
> What can man do to me?
> The Lord is on my side to help me;
> I shall look in triumph on those who hate me (*Ps.*118:5–7).

3. *Sacrifice:* He has brought a victim with him, probably to fulfil a promise he had made in his tribulation. Now he moves forward to the altar to have the sacrifice offered in public by a priest:

> O Lord, I am thy servant;
> I am thy servant, the son of thy handmaid.
> Thou hast loosed my bonds.
> I will offer to thee the sacrifice of thanksgiving
> and call on the name of the Lord.
> I will pay my vows to the Lord
> in the presence of all his people,
> in the courts of the house of the Lord,
> in your midst, O Jerusalem (*Ps.* 116:16–19).

Some of these psalms give the impression that they were composed to express the gratitude of a whole group of individuals. Since each could not narrate his own particular story of divine help and offer a separate sacrifice, one of them, or perhaps a temple priest, spoke and acted for all of them. The different elements in such a group seem to be clearly distinguished in Psalm 107.

Vv. 4–9: Thanks on behalf of those saved from the dangers of a journey through the desert.

> Then they cried to the Lord in their trouble,
> and he delivered them from their distress;
> he led them by a straight way,
> till they reached a city to dwell in (vv. 6–7).

Vv. 10–16: Thanks on behalf of those freed from prison or slavery.

> Then they cried to the Lord in their trouble,
> and he delivered them from their distress;
> he brought them out of darkness and gloom,
> and broke their bonds asunder (vv. 13–14).

Vv. 17–22: Thanks on behalf of those cured of diseases.

> they loathed any kind of food,
> and they drew near to the gates of death.
> Then they cried to the Lord in their trouble,
> and he delivered them from their distress (vv. 18–19).

Vv. 23–32: Thanks on behalf of those rescued from the perils of a sea voyage.

> Then they cried to the Lord in their trouble,
> and he delivered them from their distress;
> he made the storm be still,
> and the waves of the sea were hushed.
> Then they were glad because they had quiet,
> and he brought them to their desired haven (vv. 28–30).

Notice the use of the refrain here—"Then they cried to the Lord . . ."—probably meant to be shouted out loud and lustily by all the congregation.

Other Psalms of Personal Thanksgiving are: Psalms 18, 23, 30, 34.

Psalms of Supplication

The largest family of psalms (almost one-third of the Psalter) has as its theme a cry for help. These psalms call out to God for mercy, for assistance, in a crisis that is sometimes personal and sometimes national. We may profitably take the national or community lamentations as an example of this form of prayer. They take the shape of an urgent cry to God, reminding him of his promises to Israel, lamenting the present misery of the nation and its grave dangers, and appealing to his mercy and his past favours. From what we have seen of the history of Israel, they often had good cause for lament. These psalms are referred to as psalms of lamentation, tribulation, plaint or supplication. Almost all are from the time of the exile or later. The post-exilic psalms deal mainly with natural calamities like famine, drought or scanty harvest. The exilic lamentations bewail the fall of Jerusalem and the destruction of the temple.

A typical example is Psalm 79, which reveals the general pattern of this type of psalm. The first part of the psalm (vv. 1–7) gives the reason for the lamentation, by describing mournfully the sack of the city.

> O God, the heathen have come into thy inheritance;
> they have defiled thy holy temple;
> they have laid Jerusalem in ruins.
> They have given the bodies of thy servants
> to the birds of the air for food,
> the flesh of thy saints to the beasts of the earth.
> They have poured out their blood like water
> round about Jerusalem . . . (vv. 1–3).

The second part of the psalm (vv. 8–13) is a cry for divine mercy.

> Do not remember against us the iniquities of our forefathers;
> let thy compassion come speedily to meet us,
> for we are brought very low (v. 8).

Other psalms in this category are: Psalms 44, 60, 74, 77, 89.

It is in these Psalms of National Tribulation that we encounter the rather startling phrases that have led people to speak (incorrectly) of the Cursing Psalms. There are no cursing psalms. But there are maledictory verses included as part of a Psalm of Tribulation. When ancient Israel cried to Yahweh for help against her enemies, she did not always use the language of diplomacy to describe them. The psalms are poetry—and oriental poetry; their sentiments are expressed in the vivid imagery of all poetry, and in the passionate torrents of emotion characteristic of oriental literature. Thus we find Israel praying Yahweh to send disaster and defeat on her enemies, as, for example, in the psalm we mentioned above, Psalm 79.

> Pour out thy anger on the nations
> that do not know thee,
> and on the kingdoms
> that do not call on thy name! (v. 6).

This example indicates a first principle towards an understanding of these phrases. We must not read them in an artificial vacuum, but in the context of the whole psalm in which they occur. As in Psalm 79, the "offending verse" is much less strange to our ears when we hear it as part of an urgent appeal for the restoration of the uprooted ones of Yahweh. Perhaps we shall see this more clearly if we read Psalm 83. There, eight verses describe the Gentile conspiracy against Israel, how she is ringed about by a confederacy of enemies whose aim is expressed in verse 4:

> Come, let us wipe them out as a nation;
> let the name of Israel be remembered no more!

The second part of the psalm (vv. 9–18) prays that all these may meet the fate of Israel's enemies long ago in the days of the Judges, that they may become like the men

> who were destroyed at En-dor,
> who became dung for the ground (v. 10).

Israel prays for the annihilation of her enemies, and in this way prays that Yahweh, the God of Israel, may be recognized as almighty and supreme by all men. This is how the psalm concludes in verse 18: "Let them know that thou alone, whose name is the Lord, art the Most High over all the earth."

It is a useful exercise for us to try to look at the situation for a moment from Israel's point of view. The Israelites were the only people on the earth to whom God had committed knowledge of himself and of how he wished to be served. Only through Israel did Yahweh act in the world. Therefore, if God's plan in the world is to be accomplished, Israel must survive. But in order that she survive, the Gentiles who plot her extermination must be defeated. Thus, if God's plan of salvation is to be accomplished through Israel, he must come to Israel's aid in destroying her enemies. Because, as they saw it, the enemies of Israel were the enemies of Israel's God; as Psalm 139:21 puts it:

> Do I not hate them that hate thee, O Lord?
> And do I not loathe them that rise up against thee?

The Israelites asked God, then, to help them in destroying his enemies and theirs. And the only way they knew of destroying their enemies was by war—and war is always a bloody and a brutal thing.

We shall return to this theme in a later chapter. Here it is sufficient to say simply that Christian moral standards began with Christ. We must not expect to find them in pre-Christian times, even among the Chosen People. Only slowly and patiently did God lead men towards the high ideal of Christian charity.

How can we today still repeat these ancient maledictions? It is sobering to remember that we do express the same thoughts, but in a milder and more restrained form, whenever we ask God to grant his Church peace and security and ultimate triumph over all who oppress and persecute it. And is it not a fact that these phrases of the psalms are a primitive attempt to say, in vivid oriental language, what we express more prosaically every time we pray for the Church that the gates of hell may not prevail against it?

Pilgrimage Psalms

This is another psalm form connected with the temple and with the great public feasts in the temple calendar. Some of these psalms have, in the Psalter, the title: "A Song of Ascents", and are also called Gradual Psalms, or Caravan Songs. They were evidently composed as community marching songs, to be sung by a group of pilgrims on the way to Jerusalem for the three great feasts—Pasch, Pentecost and Tabernacles—when all good Israelites came to the temple to worship. Among the Pilgrimage Psalms are: 15, 48, 78, 121, 122. We may take Psalm 121 as a typical example.

As the caravan comes over the Judean hills, the pilgrims watch the horizon for the first glimpse of the high city of Jerusalem. The text of this psalm becomes more meaningful if we understand it as chanted by two groups of singers; it seems to have been a kind of choral dialogue. The first group begins:

> I lift up my eyes to the hills.
> From whence does my help come? (v. 1).

The answering song reminds them that Yahweh is the only source of their strength:

> My help comes from the Lord,
> who made heaven and earth (v. 2).

Then the first group chants a little prayer for the whole procession, asking Yahweh to lead them safely to their destination:

> He will not let your foot be moved,
> he who keeps you will not slumber (v. 3).

This is the Revised Standard Version rendering, but it seems more correct to put the verbs in the optative form: May he not let . . . The second group replies with verse 4, which uses the same words, but now in the form of a statement:

> Behold, he who keeps Israel
> will neither slumber nor sleep.

Thus the psalm proceeds, to conclude in verse 8 with a prayer for divine blessing on all their journeys:

> The Lord will keep
> your going out and your coming in
> from this time forth and for evermore.

How easy it is to apply this simple, natural song to lives far different from those of the Israelite pilgrims. The unlimited trust in a kindly Yahweh who knows our goings and our comings, who is ever watchful as we travel the road—this optimistic faith and hope which buoyed up the weary Israelites is surely an appropriate sentiment for all of us who travel roads more perilous than the dusty highway to Jerusalem.

Psalms as Christian Prayer

Finally, we come to the second question we set ourselves at the beginning of this chapter. Why do we, in the twentieth century, still speak to God in the words of these ancient songs, so far removed from our day and civilization, and so alien to our idiom of thought and speech? Why has the Church adopted the Jewish Book of Psalms as a handbook of Christian prayer? There are so many reasons; we can merely attempt to present a skeleton of some of them.

1. As we said already, the psalms are not merely prayers in poem form—they are inspired prayers. In using them, we use God's own words to speak to him.

2. The psalms range over the whole plan of salvation and summarize all salvation history. They provide a condensed account of Israelite history from the days of David (1000 B.C.) to the post-exilic era of the fourth century B.C. They reflect every mood of Israel's faith, and relay the voices of generations of Yahweh's worshippers. They are both a history of Israel and a history of Israel's prayer.

3. The psalms show us God's salvation plan as the Old Testament poets saw it being unfolded—in their own souls and in the nation of Israel, God's people. They are relevant now because the same salvation plan of the same God is still being unfolded in our souls and in God's new people, the Church. They are not merely snatches of antique verse fancifully adapted to a different time and theme; they are full of God now, and it is the same God, eternal and unchanging.

4. Christ not alone fulfilled the psalms' foretelling; he used them while fulfilling them. Christ grew up on the Psalter, as every Jewish boy of a good family did at the time. He learned them, he prayed them in the synagogue, he shouted Pilgrim Psalms out loud as he approached Jerusalem for the great feasts. He used the psalms in his preaching; for example, the Beatitude about the meek who shall possess the land (*Matt.* 5:5) is a quotation from Psalm 37. He recited the Hallel Psalms (*Ps.* 113–118) after the Last Supper before he went out into the moon-

lit orchard at Gethsemane. Two of the seven words on the Cross are from the psalms: "My God, my God, why hast thou forsaken me?" is the beginning of Psalm 22; his final word at death— "Into thy hands I commit my spirit" is from Psalm 31. In this way, the prayer of Israel became the prayer of Christ, and surely the prayer of Christ is the ideal prayer of Christians.

CHAPTER 12

The Closing Years

Reading: 1 Maccabees, chapters 1–16
2 Maccabees, chapters 8–15

AFTER the rebuilding of Jerusalem and the temple, the Jews settled down to normal life in a tiny enclave centred around the city. Judah has now shrunk to Judea, a rocky area within a twenty-mile radius of Jerusalem; the once proud kingdom is now an insignificant province of the vast Persian empire. And a province it is destined to remain, as empire after empire flows over the Near East. We have already traced the course of events down to about 400 B.C. All that remains is to sketch briefly the significant happenings of the final 400 years before the coming of Christ.

Hellenism

We have seen that Palestine, a narrow corridor strung along the eastern Mediterranean coastline, had always been a pathway for marching armies bent on conquest. Egyptian, Assyrian, Babylonian armies had marched through Palestine, and it had been swept helplessly into the struggle for supremacy between these giant empires. But these had all been oriental empires. Now, in the fourth century B.C., the axis of world power swings across to the European side of the Mediterranean—and remains there. And Palestine finds itself a province—first of the Greek empire of Alexander, and later of the Roman empire of Augustus. Judea makes its first real contact with Europe; and it is not difficult to see this as a providential preparation for the new "light of the Gentiles" that was soon to shine—first in Jerusalem, then in Rome, and ultimately throughout the entire world.

The picture of the oriental world around Palestine in those years is shaped and framed by the career of Alexander the Great. The Persian empire, after 200 years of ruling the known world, had grown old and tired. And it could do nothing except watch in stunned silence the meteoric rise of one of the greatest leaders the ancient world produced—the Greek Alexander the Great. This extraordinary youngster from the mountains of Macedonia was already, at the age of thirteen, a pupil of the great philosopher Aristotle. To Aristotle he owed the breadth of his scientific interests, and also his unquestioning faith in the absolute superiority of Greek civilization. His career is staggering to recall. Already an experienced general at the age of twenty, he conquered all the oriental world (and that includes Palestine) in the space of four years, and then swept southwards through present-day Persia and Afghanistan, reaching to the hitherto unknown regions of northern India, modern Pakistan. A delightful legend describes how Alexander stood weeping on the banks of the river Indus—because he could find no more worlds to conquer. His career is all the more extraordinary when we remember that he achieved all this in such a short time; he died, a victim of hard fighting and hard drinking, at the age of thirty-two. The date is 323 B.C.

It is with a summary of Alexander's conquests that the first book of Maccabees opens: "He fought many battles, conquered strongholds, and put to death the kings of the earth. He advanced to the ends of the earth, and plundered many nations. When the earth became quiet before him, he was exalted, and his heart was lifted up. He gathered a very strong army and ruled over countries, nations, and princes, and they became tributary to him" (1:2-4).

However, what made Alexander different from the other conquerors of Old Testament times was not merely his consuming energy and his far-flung victories, but his vision of a "United Nations Organization", his vision of one world bound together by Greek civilization, Greek language, Greek dress. In Alexander, as one writer puts it, "a supreme mastery of the art of war was coupled with a mystic's vision of world unity". In the wake of his armies came merchants, teachers and settlers, all Greek-speaking, bringing with them new ideas in architecture and government. All over the orient, new cities sprang up, cities in the Greek style which became outposts of Greece in this alien environment. Out of all this movement and ferment a new culture was born, neither fully Greek nor fully oriental, which we now call Hellenism (from Hellas, the ancient name for Greece). And Hellenism was not altered or disturbed by the Romans when all these cities came within their empire, so that this Hellenistic civilization provides the background to the New Testament story.

It is as a civilization rather than as a conquest that Hellenism touched tiny Judea. It presented once again, and now in a more persuasive and pernicious form, the problem with which Israel had wrestled ever since her entrance into Canaan way back in the days of Joshua—faith in Yahweh and the dangers to its survival that come from alien cultures. The Jewish heritage was an intense faith in one God and in one people of God. The new Greek culture involved Greek religion, and this was an easy-going, tolerant polytheism, a casual religion that barely disguised a supreme confidence in human ability to master all problems without reliance on any god. And thus the advantages of the Greek empire were accompanied by the hazards of Greek religious ideas. From these advantages and disadvantages flowed several results that vitally concerned Judaism—and that shaped the last Old Testament period. We shall speak about four of them: the diaspora, the Wisdom literature of the Old Testament, the Septuagint, and the Maccabean revolt.

The Diaspora

Already in the fourth century, in the final years of the Persian empire, necessity had begun to drive hundreds of Jews out of tiny and poverty-stricken Judea. The new world created by Alexander —a world centred around prosperous and exciting cities—was ideally suited to the new conditions in which the Jews found themselves. They were now, once again, a race without a nation, a landless people living chiefly by trade and handicrafts. The markets that they sought began to exist in the cities of the Hellenistic world. Secular history in the last century before Christ provides evidence of Jewish communities in all the cities around the Mediterranean coast from Rome to Alexandria. In each of these cities we find a mixed community of Jewish soldiers, goldsmiths, tentmakers, weavers, singers, philosophers, and, inevitably, beggars. Some of these Jewish colonies grew very large, such as the new seaport town of Alexandria in Egypt which came to have a Jewish population of 200,000.

In these pagan cosmopolitan cities the Jews were generally unpopular; they were disdainfully and deliberately different from their neighbours. They usually lived in their own quarter of the city, grouped around their synagogue. They kept away from the theatres and the public games so prominent a feature of Hellenism; they took no part in the state religious festivals, and closed their shops on the Sabbath. But not all pagans found them repellent. Every synagogue had its converts, pagans attracted by the Jewish fidelity to one God in a world of sceptical polytheism, attracted by the Jewish sanctity of marriage in a world of licentious domestic life. This dispersion of Jews and synagogues all around the Mediterranean coast was another of God's providential preparations for Christ and Christianity. In the first century A.D. the great traveller, St Paul, was able to go from city to city in his missionary journeys and find everywhere before him Jewish synagogues—his bridgeheads in a pagan world.

Old Testament Wisdom Literature

A type of philosophical writing called wisdom writing was common all over the orient, and is more ancient than Greek philosophy (=love of wisdom). The search for wisdom is man's way of questioning himself, his life, his destination. Wisdom takes its rise in wonder, and man, in spite of his preoccupation with the problems of survival in a world none too friendly, has always found time to wonder. Man has wondered about himself, his origin, his purpose in life, his final destination, the values of his fleeting existence. This type of speculation had long existed in Babylon and Egypt, and some of their wisdom writings have been preserved. But philosophic enquiry reached its zenith in Greece; there it became an honourable profession. Now, when Judaism moved out all over the Greek empire, it began to use this type of writing as a vehicle for its traditional ideas on the relationship between God and man, and for expressing the first stirrings of a belief in reward after death. Thus the Old Testament contains a group of books properly called Wisdom books, and now also called didactic books. They were written in this period of Hellenism and the diaspora, and many of them were written outside Judea. This wisdom literature of the Old Testament marks the final stage in the intellectual and spiritual adventure of the orient.

Some of these books, for instance Job and Ecclesiastes, are long, repetitious meditations on the inequalities of life, the suffering of the apparently innocent, and the inability of human reason to find satisfactory answers to these ever-present problems. And the unknown authors of these books have no solution to offer; the books close with a profound act of submission to God and a confession that he alone knows the pattern of his own designs. Job's last word to God is:

> I know that thou canst do all things,
> and that no purpose of thine can be thwarted . . .
> Therefore I have uttered what I did not understand,
> things too wonderful for me, which I did not know . . .
> therefore I despise myself,
> and repent in dust and ashes (*Job* 42:2, 3, 6).

Ecclesiastes concludes with the words:

> Of making many books there is no end, and much study is a weariness of the flesh. The end of the matter; all has been heard. Fear God, and keep his commandments; for this is the whole duty of man. For God will bring every deed into judgment, with every secret thing, whether good or evil (*Eccles.* 12:12–14).

Besides meditating on the profound meaning and the mysterious terminus of life, wisdom literature in the Old Testament also takes the form of a series of maxims or items of good advice. Examples of this type are the books called Ecclesiasticus, Proverbs and Wisdom, which concern themselves chiefly with giving lists of pithy sayings, proverbs, advice and instructions on practical aspects of right living, duties to parents, fellowmen, etc. Some of these pieces of advice are high-souled and sublime, others are of rather cynical earthy wisdom. One of the many examples of the first type is this passage from Ecclesiasticus 34:

The spirit of those who fear the Lord will live,
for their hope is in him who saves them.
He who fears the Lord will not be timid,
nor play the coward, for he is his hope.
Blessed is the soul of the man who fears the Lord!
To whom does he look? And who is his support?
The eyes of the Lord are upon those who love him,
a mighty protection and strong support,
a shelter from the hot wind and a shade from the noonday sun,
a guard against stumbling and a defence against falling.
He lifts up the soul and gives light to the eyes;
he grants healing, life, and blessing (vv. 13–17).

Contrast that with chapter 31 of the same book.

Eat like a human being what is set before you,
and do not chew greedily, lest you be hated.
Be the first to stop eating, for the sake of good manners,
and do not be insatiable, lest you give offence.
If you are seated among many persons,
do not reach out your hand before they do (vv. 16–18).

The Septuagint

As the Jews of the dispersion found their place in the new world of Hellenism, they ultimately required a new Old Testament language. The second-generation Jews of the diaspora grew up knowing only the Greek language, and nothing of the tongue in which their sacred books had been written. Since broad sections of the Old Testament—Law, Prophets and Psalms—were read in the synagogues, a Greek translation of the Hebrew Old Testament became a necessity. This translation, which we call the Septuagint, was completed about 140 B.C. in Alexandria. It is a symbol of the widening horizon of Judaism; such a translation into a Gentile tongue would have been unthinkable before the exile. Not alone did it satisfy the needs of the emigrant Jews, but it also opened to the surrounding pagan world the hidden treasures of the inspired books. But its real function in the scheme of salvation was something that its translators could not have foreseen. It became the Old Testament used by the first Christian communities; it was the Old Testament quoted by St Paul and all the early preachers; with its help they demonstrated to the Greek-speaking world that Christ had fulfilled the ancient promises of the Old Testament. It is thus one more step in God's patient preparation of the world scene for the entry of the Messiah and his universal salvation message.

The Maccabees

While all this was happening throughout the empire, back in Judea Hellenism took its most unpleasant form. There the tension between the new Greek culture and the strict religion of the Judean Jews was bound to explode into open opposition. Things came to a head due to the cruelty of one of the princes who succeeded to a part of Alexander's empire, a man called Antiochus IV. Palestine came under his rule in 175 B.C. He was an obstinate and determined apostle of Hellenism, and he demanded unconditional submission to the great Greek god, Zeus. Naturally, no policy could have been better calculated to stir up trouble in Judea.

Antiochus outraged the Jews by attempting to turn Jerusalem into a Greek city. He built a gymnasium for the pagan games—and built it near the temple, and when this was not Hellenizing the Jews effectively enough, Antiochus turned tyrant. He forbade, under pain of death, the honoured observances of the Mosaic covenant—circumcision, Sabbath and sacrifice. He confiscated their copies of the Old Testament and burnt them publicly. He looted their beloved temple, and—final horror—set up on the altar of holocausts a statue of the pagan god Zeus. This full-scale religious persecution is described in 1 Maccabees 1:21–67; in reading these verses you will taste the bitterness of the Jews' shock and sorrow. What began as an imposition of an alien culture ended as a purely religious persecution, and when it turned religious, the Jews revolted. Thus began the Maccabean insurrection, the final fight for freedom in the chequered history of the Old Testament.

The insurrection began as the revolt of a single family, a man called Mattathias and his five sons. Mattathias was a priest in the little village of Modein, twenty miles north-west of Jerusalem. To this remote village came the officers of Antiochus demanding that all sacrifice to Zeus. Mattathias refused, gathered around him a group of devout Jews with the cry: "Let every one who is zealous for the law and supports the covenant come out with me!" (1 *Macc.* 2:27)—and fled into the Judean hills. They were joined by many Jews from Jerusalem, and carried on guerrilla warfare against the king's agents until the death of Mattathias in 167 B.C.

His son Judas became leader. He was a gifted military leader, and under his command the Jews became an army. This army Judas led in a gallant but unequal struggle against the might of an empire and against many apostate Jews. He inflicted so many unexpected defeats on the enemy that he earned the name Maccabeus, "the Hammerer", the title by which he—and the whole campaign—would be remembered. The two books of Maccabees centre around him and his exploits.

Judas Maccabeus led the revolt for only six years (he was killed in battle in 161 B.C.), but in that time he succeeded in winning back to the Jews the city of Jerusalem. 1 Maccabees 4 describes the cleansing of the profaned temple and altar; read this chapter in order to savour the joy and zeal of the last religious rebels of Judaism. Chapter 8 tells how, just before his untimely death, Judas Maccabeus made a league of friendship with the

Romans: "Now Judas heard of the fame of the Romans, that they were very strong and were well-disposed towards all who made an alliance with them, that they pledged friendship to those who came to them, and that they were very strong" (v. 1).

The Roman empire was taking shape at this time, and would soon overrun the whole Mediterranean seaboard. Judas felt it politically prudent to make the Romans his friends, and chapter 8 concludes with the text of the treaty his ambassadors made with them. However, this league with Rome really contributed nothing to the Jewish cause, because the Romans did not come to help the Maccabees in their fight for freedom. And when the Romans did finally come to Judea—under Pompey in 63 B.C.—they came as conquerors, not as liberators.

There is a note of deep sadness in the simple words that narrate the death of Judas in battle.

> Then Jonathan and Simon took Judas their brother and buried him in the tomb of their fathers at Modein, and wept for him. And all Israel made great lamentation for him; they mourned many days and said,
> > "How is the mighty fallen,
> > the saviour of Israel!" (1 *Macc.* 9: 19-21).

His two brothers, Jonathan and Simon, succeeded him in turn, and brought the Maccabean revolt to a reasonably successful conclusion. Of course, the greatest single blessing for the struggling Jews of this period was the death of the tyrant Antiochus. His departure from the stage, together with the efforts of Jonathan and Simon, gave to the Jews the religious freedom they had set out to win.

Simon was the last of the Maccabee family to lead his people. 1 Maccabees 14:35 tells us: "The people saw Simon's faithfulness and the glory which he had resolved to win for his nation, and they made him their leader and high priest . . ." This combination of political and priestly power in a single person was a disastrous marriage of incompatibles, and it laid the foundation for the sorry and corrupt state of the high priesthood that we encounter at the time of Christ. Simon's son, John Hyrcanus, in-

herited both the civil and religious authority of his father, and
inaugurated the last dynasty of Judea—the Hasmonean dynasty.
These kings were really subordinates of the ruling empire, but
they were local kings. This Hasmonean dynasty continued from
the death of John Hyrcanus (103) up to 37 B.C., when a crafty
adventurer called Herod, from the desert of Idumea, induced
the Roman Senate to appoint him king. He became Herod the
Great, the man who called himself king of Judea when another
and greater king of the Jews was born one night in Bethlehem.

Significance of the Struggle

We have said enough to show that the Maccabean rising is the
key event in the period that brings the Old Testament to a close.
In spite of the apparent hopelessness of their struggle, Mattathias
and his sons achieved the inauguration of the last Jewish kingdom. This revolt gave Judea a native Jewish dynasty for almost a
century. More important, it gave the Jews freedom to practise
their religion undisturbed—a freedom that the Romans never
took away from them. The splendour of the old Davidic kingdom
never returned, but Jerusalem and its temple stood again at the
heart of Judaism. In short, the Maccabean insurrection brought
into being the Jewish world that we find at the coming of Christ.

For information about Judea during the final century before
his coming we rely on the Jewish historian, Josephus Flavius. The
picture he paints, even allowing for exaggerations, is alarmingly
sombre. During the Hasmonean dynasty, the two groups,
"Pharisees" and "Sadducees", emerged, and moved rapidly into
violent hostility. The Pharisees held rigidly to the law of Moses,
but buried it under a multiplicity of rules and interpretations. The
Sadducees were more a political party than a religious group, and
saw little difficulty in combining the traditions of Israel with the
culture of Hellenism. The struggle between these two groups was
a prolonged and bitter civil war, and produced some grim
ironies. On one occasion a Jewish king hired foreign mercenaries
to slaughter his fellow-Jews, and paid them by plundering the
tomb of King David. Again, the Pharisees, in their bitterness

against king and Sadducees, called for help on an outsider—a descendant of the hated Antiochus IV. When the king finally triumphed, he crucified 800 Pharisees outside Jerusalem.

That so many Jews remained good and faithful servants of Yahweh, their God, in such monstrous circumstances is ultimately due to the radiance of the Maccabees' fidelity to the religion of their fathers. Their revolt was the last bid for freedom of faith and country that the Old Testament witnessed. And in a sense it recapitulated all that had gone before, and it stands as a final symbol from pre-Christian times of the struggle of true religion against all the forces that threaten it everywhere. It began as a family resistance movement and spread into a holy war of national independence. In much the same way, the Old Testament story began as a family migration—Abraham and his clan—and widened into a nation of believers. However mixed the motives that inspired Jews to rally to the Maccabean guerrillas in the hills, the outcome of the rebellion was not a free Judea but a free worship of Yahweh. In this, too, it is a picture in miniature of the whole Old Testament, in which Jewish hopes of earthly empire are repeatedly shattered, but in which men are all the time being guided forward towards a kingdom which "is not of this world".

There is hardly any doubt that this final desperate struggle against the power of an empire and against religious tyranny, this last heroic martyrdom of some of Judaism's noblest sons, did much to restore to the harrassed community of Judea something of the old crusading spirit that had sustained Moses in the wilderness, that had carried Joshua across the Jordan, that had inspired the religious revival of Josiah, that had led Nehemiah and Ezra back from Babylon to triumph over poverty and despair. And this renewed spirit of zeal for Yahweh and attachment to his covenant kept a little cluster of Jews together around the temple during the silent years—about which the Bible tells us nothing—the 130 years between the end of the Books of Maccabees and the opening chapter of the Gospels.

CHAPTER 13

Men and Morals

THE morality of the Old Testament is a subject that people sometimes find mysterious, often exasperating, but always intriguing. The modern Christian conscience tends to find this subject a little embarrassing also, and the first reaction sometimes is to search for an excuse for our erring Old Testament heroes. We hope to show that such a search for excuses is both fruitless and unnecessary, and to suggest that what we need is not an excuse but an attitude of mind, namely an understanding of the historical and theological background to Old Testament life and legislation. In other words, our concern is to explain the Old Testament viewpoint, not to explain it away.

We need not waste time here with the quaint opinion that some passages in the Old Testament are unedifying and better omitted. St Paul, who knew and understood the Old Testament much better than we do, told Timothy: "*All* scripture is inspired by God and profitable for teaching, for reproof, for correction, and for training in righteousness, that the man of God may be complete, equipped for every good work" (2 *Tim.* 3:16–17). This introduces a more important issue: the inspired writers do not seem perturbed by the incidents that tend to raise twentieth-century eyebrows. They sing the praises of the great figures in Israel's history, but at the same time make no attempt to disguise their weaknesses and failures.

What we have seen of Old Testament history is sufficient to show us that an attitude of outraged piety fits badly with the biblical facts, and that our task is to find ourselves a broader and more scriptural vision. We attempt the impossible when we try to examine morality as an isolated abstraction; we must take account of the men as well as the morals of the Old Testament. And this means keeping in mind the historical perspective. Since the religion and morality of the Israelite nation spring from, and depend on, the Sinai covenant, the Bible naturally regards Moses as the founder of Israel's religion. But, in the text of Genesis, Israel's history and faith begin with Abraham. As Genesis crosses over from pre-history into the historical era at chapter 12, we find Abraham standing there as the ultimate ancestor of Israel's religion. In fact, the religion of the patriarchs is the only reason why we are interested in them rather than in the thousands of nameless semi-nomads who roamed the Fertile Crescent in the second millennium B.C.

Pre-Mosaic Morality

Because of the penury of our knowledge, it is impossible to describe the religion and morality of the patriarchs in detail, but from the Genesis account it was clearly a type of religion which was at home in the world of their day. That Abraham's ancestors had been polytheistic pagans is clear from archeology, and is affirmed by the Bible itself. "Your fathers lived of old beyond the Euphrates, Terah, the father of Abraham and of Nahor; and they served other gods" (*Jos.* 24:2).

The religion of the patriarchs appears in Genesis as an intensely personal one—a relationship between a man and his God. As far as we know, no moral laws were attached to this new religion, and so the patriarchs followed the code of behaviour accepted at the time—a code which we are only slowly piecing together.

This relationship between a man and his God centred around vocation, covenant and promise; a man is called by God, makes a covenant with God, is promised a reward by God. God's promise to Abraham is presented as the chief motive-force in Abraham's life. This promise is of land and posterity: ". . . all the land which you see I will give to you and to your descendants for ever. I will make your descendants as the dust of the earth; so that if one can count the dust of the earth, your descendants also can be counted" (*Gen.* 13:15–16).

The same promise is repeated many times. We miss the significance of this promise unless we remember that the nomad desires nothing more ardently than land and posterity. For the nomad, land and posterity mean survival. Abraham, Isaac and Jacob were wandering tribal chieftains, and their religious beliefs and practices were coloured by nomadic tribal conditions.

As we said in talking about Abraham, the tribal family was a small, compact unit that moved from place to place with flocks of sheep and goats. Nomads had no fixed abode; they were ever and everywhere strangers. The land they grazed was never theirs; they had always to be ready to move on, if the local inhabitants showed signs of hostility. Theirs was an itinerant problem. Permanent homes, walled towns, cultivated vineyards—all these were outside their experience, beyond their reach. Hence the nomad's deep desire for a land of his own, a permanent home of his own. As wanderers, perpetual trespassers, the nomad and his family were ever in danger of extinction. An enemy raid (as that described in Genesis 14), the accumulated hostility of the surrounding settlers, even a single rash incident, could involve the tribal unit in an unequal struggle against an enemy who could obliterate it. Jacob voices this fear in Genesis 34:30: "You have brought trouble on me by making me odious to the inhabitants of the land, the Canaanites and the Perizzites; my numbers are few, and if they gather themselves against me and attack me, I shall be destroyed, both I and my household."

From this situation comes the constant necessity of increasing the tribe, of perpetuating the structure. The later Israelite desire for fruitful wives and many children springs from this tribal origin.

The survival and security of the tribe demanded, ultimately, land and posterity. And when land and posterity are also the object of a divine promise, then the patriarchs' natural desire for them is shot through with a religious fervour. Land and posterity now take on the nature of a divinely-appointed goal. Land and posterity now mean, not alone the survival and security of the tribe, but the transmission of the true worship of God. Anything that threatens the fulfilment of the divine promise must be overcome, not merely for natural reasons, but for a supernatural reason, which is that the true religion may be perpetuated. It is in the light of all this that we must judge the actions of the patriarchs. Their actions reflect, in some way or other, a desire to attain the promised children and land, so that God's people may increase and multiply. The question of their survival was one of natural and religious urgency.

Jacob's Lie

Probably no moral problem in the patriarchal story has so teased readers as the incident in Genesis 27, in which Jacob, by consummate fraud, robs his brother Esau of their father's death-bed blessing. You should read this delightful chapter immediately. Jacob is pushed forward by that rather familiar figure, a scheming and ambitious mother, who arranged to cook Isaac's favourite menu and to dress Jacob in sufficient woollies to be mistaken for his hairy brother. Genesis 27 has been a stumbling-block for so many embarrassed exegetes that it may be worth squandering a few moments on some of the early and hopeless attempts to deal with it. The dilemma has always been: either admit that Jacob told a lie—but then explain how God rewards him; or deny that he told a lie—but then explain the text of Genesis 27.

The earliest avenue of escape was—the end justifies the means; lying is permissible if circumstances render it necessary. At the beginning of the third century Origen wrote: "A man who has to lie should imitate the patriarch Jacob, who, we read, got his blessing by the trick of a lie." Several heretics adopted Origen's convenient explanation and taught that, following Jacob, a Christian could deny his faith if necessary to save his life! It was to oppose this error that St Augustine wrote a book called "Against Lying", in which he described Jacob's conduct by a famous phrase: *Non est mendacium, sed mysterium* (It is not a lie, but a mystery). He argued thus: Jacob's words can be called a lie only in the literal sense; but he was not speaking literally. Under the inspiration of the holy Spirit he was speaking in language figurative and mystical. He put on goatskins, as a type of sin, to signify the Messiah who took on the sins of others. In saying that he was the firstborn he was mystically foreshadowing the casting out of the Jews and the substitution of the Gentiles. Augustine concludes: "If these are lies, then all parables, types and figurative speech must be called lies; which is nonsense." In this way St Augustine felt that he had rather skilfully excised the lie from the story.

His solution was accepted with joy and buttressed with new arguments by some of the greatest names in Christian writing. The objections of less famous men—that this was a historical incident to be judged in its Old Testament context—found little hearing. All opposition was scornfully brushed aside by St Albert the Great, who said: "The counsels of the holy Spirit should not be spoken about rashly, but rather ought we to venerate them in silence."

Difficulties were meant to be solved, not venerated in silence, and gradually scholars began to desert Augustine and admit that Jacob could, and did, lie. But the success that crowned his lie continued to raise a question-mark. One theologian absolved Jacob by throwing all the blame on Rebecca. Women, according to him, are wonderful at simulation and deceit. "O unhappy men," he wrote, "who daily are deceived and bluffed by wives to whom they have surrendered themselves into slavery. I see no more apt symbol of this misery than Isaac." A famous moral theologian, Lessius, proposed Jacob as the earliest recorded user of a mental reservation. Outwardly, Jacob said he was Esau, but inwardly he added: as far as dignity is concerned! However, by the nineteenth century a more sensible approach had become universal. One commentator of that period says crisply: "Even though Augustine was a learned philosopher, it is only too obvious that Jacob lied."

This diversion into early and medieval exegesis is not entirely irrelevant. We can at least learn from the errors of our predecessors. The moral to be drawn in this case is: the hopelessness of seeking a solution on any except the historical and textual plane, the futility of taking refuge in symbolic or imaginary meanings. We recognize now that an evaluation of the morality of the Old

Testament must be made in terms of the historical circumstances, and with the information supplied by the text itself, not springing from the fertility of our imaginations. And even if we cannot offer a satisfactory solution we at least know some of the mistakes to be avoided.

So, keeping to the text, what have we to say today about the Jacob incident? We agree with St Augustine that it is a mystery, but we must insist that it is also a lie. In fact, Jacob told four lies in rapid succession: verse 19 (two), and verses 20 and 24 (*Gen.* 27). Now, we do not necessarily accept this dialogue as a faithful re-production of what took place historically; ancient history, sacred and secular, tended to compose dialogue to help describe a historical encounter. But the little drama certainly enshrines an act of duplicity and deceit, and reflects no credit on Jacob. And he does not seem to have acted in blissful ignorance; verse 12 makes him say: "Perhaps my father will feel me, and I shall seem to be mocking him, and bring a curse upon myself and not a blessing." Nor did he consider later that his deed had gone un-punished. "Thus I was; by day the heat consumed me, and the cold by night, and my sleep fled from my eyes. These twenty years I have been in your house; I served you fourteen years for your two daughters, and six years for your flock, and you have changed my wages ten times." (*Gen.* 31:40-1).

However, the most important point that the text produces is: God's election of Jacob over Esau was not the result of Jacob's petty ruse. If you read Genesis 25:21-26 you will see that, in the mind of the authors of the Pentateuch, this was a free choice by God, and thus the whole incident becomes just one more example of God making use of even the frailty of men to accomplish his designs. And, of course, we must always remember that God's choice of a man does not automatically mean God's approval of all that this man does.

Israel at Sinai

We have said that the Bible regards Moses as the founder of Israel's religion. He was the great leader and legislator whose in-

13

fluence over Israel's life and faith continued all through the Old Testament. Around the nucleus of the Sinai Decalogue there grew up gradually a detailed code of behaviour, moral and ritual. The Old Testament, then, is a recording of doctrinal and moral growth—of God adapting himself to the religious ideas and progress of the people of his choice. The divine teaching must, at each step of the way, be placed in its historical setting. And this is true of the beginnings with Moses.

God did not create a special race of men, perfect, upright and enlightened, to be his people. He chose an existing race, at a specific moment in its history. Divine election is not a creation; God chose the Israelites as they were then. They had, at the time of Sinai, a fund of ideas, religious and moral, many of which were imperfect and some of which were incorrect. God used these ideas as a starting-point, and worked on them patiently to perfect the imperfect and eliminate the incorrect. Their ideas of warfare were as simple and as ruthless as those of their neighbours; their ideas of justice reflected their stage of cultural development. But this was the Israel that God had chosen.

Slavery

One of the social institutions of Israel at that time was slavery. And slavery continued, just as it continued as a social and economic factor all around Israel in the successive empires, Assyrian, Babylonian, Persian, Greek and Roman. Traffic in slaves was general throughout the ancient East, and the Mosaic law allowed Israelites to buy non-Israelites as slaves. ". . . you may buy male and female slaves from among the nations that are round about you" (*Lev.* 25:44).

Israelites themselves could be reduced to slavery only by their own poverty; generally they were defaulting debtors. For example, in 2 Kings 4 the prophet Elisha performs a miracle to help a poor woman whose two children are about to be taken as slaves by a creditor. Besides, Israelites could not be enslaved permanently—they had to be set free on the Jubilee Year, which occurred every seventh year.

In everyday life, the lot of a slave depended largely on the character of his master, but the Mosaic law ensured him a minimum of rights. He really formed a member of the family; thus he had to observe the Sabbath rest and share in the religious feasts. Many slaves seem to have been trusted servants; for instance, it was to his slave that Abraham confided the task of finding a wife for his son Isaac (*Gen.* 24). The following passage from Ecclesiasticus probably gives a reliable picture of the Israelites' attitude to their domestic slaves, at least in later Old Testament times. The lights and shadows of slavery are all there.

> Fodder and a stick and burden for an ass;
> bread and discipline and work for a servant.
> Set your slave to work, and you will find rest;
> leave his hands idle, and he will seek liberty.
> Yoke and thong will bow the neck,
> and for a wicked servant there are racks and tortures.
> Set him to work, as is fitting for him,
> and if he does not obey, make his fetters heavy.
> Do not act immoderately towards anybody,
> and do nothing without discretion.
> If you have a servant, treat him as a brother . . ."
>
> (*Ecclus.* 33:24–31)

In general, the picture of slavery in Israel shows that, while the custom was retained and legalized, the treatment of slaves was more favourable than, for example, in the Roman empire. And in Israel there never existed those enormous slave-gangs that were a feature of the empire. Nor was the position of a slave ever so low in Israel as in republican Rome, where a slave was defined as "a kind of talking instrument".

War

Having been chosen by God, Israel became a nation—and a holy nation. It was holy in the Old Testament sense of the word, that is consecrated to God, belonging to Yahweh alone. As the Israelites saw it, God's purpose in choosing them was that they

should invoke his name and proclaim it; they alone recognized
the existence of the one true God, and they would ultimately
bear witness to him before all the peoples of the earth. From this
they drew the quite logical conclusion that the continued physical
survival of Israel in the purity of her worship of Yahweh was
essential to Yahweh's purpose. That is why Israel believed so
fiercely in the indefectibility of the nation. That is why the prayer
of Israel, the Psalter, continually reminds God that he must save
Israel for the sake of his own name. That is why the psalms can
pray with such vehemence for the destruction of Israel's enemies
—because, as we said already, the enemies of Israel were the
enemies of the God of Israel. That is why the Israelites can
attack Canaan with such fury—because this was the land Yahweh
had promised them, and in taking possession of it, in the only
way they knew, they were implementing his divine will. This
promised land was to be the home of a "people holy to the Lord
your God" (*Deut.* 7:6); a place where Israel could keep the law of
Yahweh perfectly. But this cannot be done unless all the tribes
to be found in Canaan were destroyed, because they were all
polytheistic idolators—a perpetual obstacle to the true religion.
Thus, the entry into Canaan should involve the destruction of the
nations living there. This is the basis for what is called the law of
herem, commanding the total extermination of an enemy.

The Hebrew word "herem" means to separate, to put something apart for sacred use—forbidden to men and consecrated to
God. As applied to war, it meant leaving to God the fruits of
victory. In theory, as expressed in Deuteronomy, the law of
herem seems to admit of no exception. ". . . when the Lord your
God gives them over to you, and you defeat them; then you must
utterly destroy them; you shall make no covenant with them, and
show no mercy to them" (7:2).

The reason is given in verse 16: ". . . your eye shall not pity
them; neither shall you serve their gods, for that would be a
snare to you."

In practice, however, we must seriously question whether
these prescriptions were in fact applied. They seem to have been
observed in specific localized instances, as at Jericho (*Jos.* 6:21),

but there are many indications that this law of herem was not taken literally by the Israelites.

The text of Deuteronomy 7 itself, having commanded complete destruction, goes on to forbid inter-marriage with the conquered pagans. "You shall not make marriages with them, giving your daughters to their sons or taking their daughters for your sons. For they would turn away your sons from following me, to serve other gods . . ." (vv. 3–4).

The law of verse 3 is surely unnecessary if the law of verse 2 had been observed. Again, a repetition of the law of herem in Deuteronomy 20:13–17 commands that only the male population be put to death. In fact, because they did not obey this law, the Israelites tottered again and again to the brink of idolatry, drawn by the example of the pagans they had allowed to survive among them. Taking these and similar facts into account, several scholars nowadays regard the law of herem expressed in Deuteronomy as a statement of an attitude of mind rather than a command to be obeyed literally. They see it as a colourful and dramatic oriental way of saying: it would be better for you to exterminate your enemies, as other nations do, than allow them to infect your religion. Thus, it is rather like Christ's phrase in Matthew 5:29: "If your right eye causes you to sin, pluck it out and throw it away." Nobody considers that this is to be taken literally as a command to self-mutilation; it is an expression of what our attitude to temptation should be.

The picture of Israelite warfare that the Old Testament gives us shows that, while the Israelites fell below the New Testament standards of morality (and this is only natural), they were still rising slowly above the wartime ethics of the neighbouring nations. Captured enemies were not subjected to prolonged public torture by the Israelites as they were by the Assyrian kings. There are signs that the Israelites, while remaining children of their time, were being guided towards the far-off ideal. Besides, as Fr John McKenzie remarks, "it is not seemly for a world which has evolved the concept of total war to point the finger at Joshua and his Hebrews." We have no desire to excuse them, but we have an obligation to understand them. And when we do try to

understand them, perhaps we can agree with the conclusion of
the American scholar, Albright: "It is questionable whether a
strictly detached observer would consider it (Joshua's slaughter
of the Canaanites) as bad as the starvation of helpless Germany
after the armistice in 1918 or the bombing of Rotterdam in 1940."
And these incidents took place after two millennia of Christianity.

Social Morality

The moral standards of a people are best illustrated, not from
times of great national crisis, but from day-to-day living and
social contacts. For the Israelites, every aspect of private and
social life was governed by the Decalogue. Around the Decalogue
as a core, there grew up the Code of the Alliance and the multiplicity of legal prescriptions found in Exodus, Leviticus and
Deuteronomy. This body of moral law involved more than external acts—it demanded an inner spirit. It governed relationships
between man and man, and not merely with reference to the good
of society. More important, it assumed as fundamental that each
man enjoys the love and protection of God, the Father of all.
From this assumption sprang the Israelites' attitude to the poor,
to widows, to orphans—an attitude that is one of the shining
lights of Old Testament morality. As a sample of such legislation,
read Deuteronomy 24:12–22. However, concerning the social
structure of their morality, two aspects deserve mention: the law
of retaliation and the marriage legislation.

Law of Retaliation

This is mentioned by Christ in Matthew 5:38: "You have
heard that it was said, 'An eye for an eye and a tooth for a tooth.'"
It is expressed in all its crudity in Exodus 21:23–25: ". . . you
shall give life for life, eye for eye, tooth for tooth, hand for hand,
foot for foot, burn for burn, wound for wound, stripe for stripe."
However, we seem to have here a situation similar to that in the
Deuteronomy text of the law of herem. The context of Exodus 21
casts grave doubt on the literal application of this law of revenge.

First, it is preceded by a law which orders, as punishment for a wound inflicted in a fight, not a similar wound, but financial compensation. "When men quarrel and one strikes the other with a stone or with his fist and the man does not die but keeps his bed, then if the man rises again and walks abroad with his staff, he that struck him shall be clear; only he shall pay for the loss of his time, and shall have him thoroughly healed" (vv. 18–19). Secondly, the law of revenge is followed by a ruling which orders the liberation of a slave in compensation for loss of eye, or even tooth (v. 26). In fact, in only one case in the Mosaic law do we find strict application to the law of retaliation, and that is in the case of murder, where Deuteronomy 19 insists on life for life. And this is explained in the text by a religious reason: the blood which has been shed has profaned the land in which Yahweh dwells. Therefore the conclusion emerges that the law of retaliation is an emphatic and Semitic way of asserting the principle of proportionate compensation. In any case, even at its worst, it provides a kind of rough-and-ready justice; it is an attempt to curb the instinct for revenge by keeping it within observable limits.

Concept of Marriage

Genesis 2 presents monogamous marriage as a divine institution, and thereby as the will of God. In Matthew 19, Christ says that he is restoring marriage to its original condition, and explicitly asserts that, during the Old Testament period, "for the hardness of your heart Moses allowed you to divorce your wives". What picture does the Old Testament itself give us of marriage under the Mosaic code?

Deuteronomy 21:15, in legislating for the inheritance of a father's property, recognizes bigamy as a legal fact. And we have already mentioned that kings sometimes kept a large harem. Not that the law gave them special rights; simply, this was a luxury which few could afford, and it thus became the privilege of kings. Apart from kings, it seems that the most common form of marriage in Israel was monogamy. It is striking that the books of Samuel and Kings, which cover the entire period of the monarchy from 1000 to 586 B.C., do not record a single case of bigamy outside the royal family. Similarly, the wisdom literature, which provides a picture of Israelite society in post-exilic times, never mentions polygamy. The prophets use the image of a monogamous marriage to represent Israel as the one wife chosen by the one true God.

Deuteronomy 24:1 gives a husband the right to divorce his wife, and the reason mentioned there is: "if she finds no favour in his eyes because he has found some indecency in her". This vague expression was interpreted in very different ways by different rabbinical schools. Some said that only adultery was sufficient cause; others would accept even trivial reasons, for instance that she allowed her husband's dinner to burn. From this we can conclude that the divorce law was accepted in a rather generous sense.

The form of divorce was simple: the husband made out a written declaration saying that she was no longer his wife. This is the "bill of divorce" or "bill of repudiation". The possession of this document by the woman allowed her to marry again. The divorce law was of benefit only to the husband—women could not ask for a divorce. We are quite unable to calculate how common divorce was in the Old Testament.

In speaking about the Decalogue we mentioned that the Israelites understood the sixth commandment to forbid only the taking of another man's wife. And this they regarded chiefly as a violation of her husband's property. The punishment for adultery was death by stoning of both the guilty parties (*Lev.* 20:10).

Over against this restricted application of the sixth commandment we must set the truly remarkable attitude of the Old Testament towards modesty as the safeguard of chastity. On this subject the wisdom literature is full of gems of good advice; Ecclesiasticus 9 is typical.

> Do not associate with a woman singer,
> lest you be caught in her intrigues . . .
> Turn away your eyes from a shapely woman,
> and do not look intently at beauty belonging to another.

Never dine with another man's wife,
nor revel with her at wine ... (vv. 4; 8–9).

Even accidental nudity was reproved:

And you shall not go up by steps to my altar, that your
nakedness be not exposed on it. (*Exod.* 20:26).

Prostitution was certainly not encouraged:

Do not profane your daughter by making her a harlot, lest the
land fall into harlotry and the land become full of wickedness.
(*Lev.* 19:29).

Religious or temple prostitution, part of the ritual of all her
pagan neighbours, was completely banned in Israel.

Israelite Religion

To have a sympathetic understanding of Old Testament
morality we must know something of Old Testament religion.
Now, what constituted religion for the Israelites?

They regarded themselves as covenanted to the Lord, and
fidelity to the covenant was the core of their religion. Old Testament religion is concerned with the call of God and the response
of man. God speaks to man, and man listens, accepts and obeys.
This is what constitutes perfection for man—his relationship to
God, rather than the way he corresponds to a human ideal of
morality. This is why Genesis and Paul can agree that Abraham
"believed the Lord; and he reckoned it to him as righteousness"
(*Gen.* 15:6—cited five times in the New Testament).

This does not mean that God ignores morality, or is satisfied
with faulty moral standards. It means simply that, in this as in
all other spheres, God is patient and understanding enough to
adapt his call to the concrete human and historical situation. What
is constant in Old Testament religion is the demand that one
should submit to God's call, whatever it may be. And what is
important at any given moment is not the resulting improvement
in human ideals, but the humility and faith with which man

responds to that call of God. We may find fault with many details of Abraham's moral conduct, but to the demands that God did make on him—to be a wanderer in an alien land, to put his long-awaited son on an altar for sacrifice—to these demands he responded with wholehearted unquestioning submission.

The imperfections as well as the glory of Old Testament religion are put in their proper perspective by St Paul when he says that "the law was our custodian until Christ came" (*Gal.* 3:24). "Custodian" translates a Greek word which in Hellenistic circles meant the family servant who led a boy safely into manhood. St Paul is simply saying that the function of the Old Testament was to lead humanity to the maturity of the Christian way of life. Out of the imperfections of the old alliance God, through Christ and his Church, would make all things new. There is truth as well as poetry in the Church's chant, *O felix culpa* (O happy fault); God still shows himself capable of bringing good, even out of evil.

As we grow in understanding and appreciation of the Old Testament, we come to realize that it needs no excuses. The Old Testament is the story of mankind, and we should have little difficulty in recognizing our brothers there. Abraham was a crude and unwashed desert chieftain, but, as far as he understood God's demands on him, he responded fully. Jacob was a shrewd and resourceful Bedouin, but all through a turbulent life he held fast to the God of his fathers. Joshua lacked our ideal of charity, but by waging war on Israel's enemies he was fighting for faith and fatherland. David fell for Bathsheba, but when God sent the prophet Nathan to recall him, David returned like the Prodigal Son. In other words, it was to people like us that God spoke in the Old Testament; it was people like us who were called, and who responded. Besides describing the Christians of Corinth, St Paul was summarizing the whole salvation story when he wrote: ". . . God chose what is foolish in the world to shame the wise, God chose what is weak in the world to shame the strong, God chose what is low and despised in the world, even things that are not, to bring to nothing things that are, so that no human being might boast in the presence of God" (1 *Cor.* 1:27–9).

Looking Back

LOOKING back across the Old Testament we can now see how the bits and pieces of its history fall into place. We can see how this long story was a God-designed preparation for a new David and a new kingdom of Yahweh—a David who would be a divine king, and a kingdom that would be everlasting. Perhaps we can now savour something of the wonder of it all—the wonder that so frail a flower could have survived the harsh winds of oriental imperialism. The story began with Abraham, a solitary witness to Yahweh, a man who roamed unfriendly pastures and died without leaving a footprint on the sands of political history. Who, humanly speaking, could have foreseen that the descendants of this wandering goatherd would carve out for themselves the little kingdom of Israel, and build a proud city and temple on the Judean hillsides where he once grazed his flocks? And what force except Yahweh's patient love could have transformed a grumbling mob of slaves in the Nile delta in the thirteenth century into the psalm-singing pilgrims of the second temple in the fifth century?

We have also developed some sense of involvement in this ancient history. As we said at the very beginning, this is not the story of the salvation of others; it is the story of our salvation. The love of God and the knowledge of God that illumine our lives have come to us from and through the Old Testament. This story of Yahweh's constant love and man's fickle response, this story of frailty, fall, repentance and final triumph is the story of the people of God. And it continues to be the story of the new people of God, Christ's Church. More than that, it is the story of each individual among this people of God. There is a sense in which it is true to say that one could hand a Bible to any man and tell him: This is your life!

However, the principal impression in our minds as we reach the end of the Old Testament is a keen consciousness that it is an incomplete drama, an unfinished symphony. We have watched this people grow from a single patriarch into the kingdom of David. As we mentioned already, they went through the successive stages of being a family, a people, a nation, a kingdom and a church. But the Old Testament ends with the Jews scattered all over the Roman empire, and a hard core of zealous ones huddled in the shadow of the second Jerusalem temple, dependent on a high priest who has become a political speculator. This is no fitting conclusion to a story that began so splendidly with the blessing given to Abraham: "I will make you exceedingly fruitful; and I will make nations of you, and kings shall come forth from you. And I will establish my covenant between me and you and your descendants after you throughout their generations for an everlasting covenant, to be God to you and to your descendants after you" (*Gen.* 17:6–7).

This is no fulfilment of the promise made to David: "And your house and your kingdom shall be made sure for ever before me; your throne shall be established for ever" (2 *Sam.* 7:16).

Surely this does not satisfy the splendid vision of Jeremiah: "I will put my law within them, and I will write it upon their hearts; and I will be their God, and they shall be my people ... for I will forgive their iniquity, and I will remember their sin no more" (*Jer.* 31:33–4).

In this way, we can clearly see that the Old Testament—and all the great figures in it—are really the finger of God pointing towards the New Testament. The Old Testament is all the time directing our gaze to something outside and beyond itself—to a greater and a brighter future. Only in the incarnation and redemption does the Old Testament reach its destination. It was the Advent season of humanity, the long vigil for the Messiah. It looked forward to an event that would be, not merely an epilogue, but an explanation of the whole; not merely a conventional happy ending, but the climax, the focal point of everything. This was what St Paul was thinking of when he told the Romans: "For Christ is the end of the law" (10:4).

Many times throughout the Old Testament Yahweh rescued his children from exile—of various kinds. Through Moses, he brought them out from Egypt, through Joshua he led them in from the desert, through the prophets he recalled them from sin, through Nehemiah he reinstated the remnant from Babylon. But only through Christ did he finally and definitively set all his exiles free.